Collecting
Victorian
Jewelry

Identification and Price Guide

C. Jeanenne Bell, G.G.

Published by

kp books

An imprint of F+W Publications, Inc.

700 East State Street • Iola, WI 54990-0001
715-445-2214 • 888-457-2873

Our toll-free number to place an order or obtain
a free catalog is (800) 258-0929.

Library of Congress Catalog Number: 2004093888
ISBN: 0-87349-673-6

Designed by Wendy Wendt
Edited by Mary Sieber

Printed in United States of America

Dedication

Dedicated to the One from Whom all things cometh;

my parents, Anne and Belton Noblitt;

my parents-in-law, Theda and Jim Hess;

my husband, Michael Marshall;

and my four children and 10 grandchildren.

Contents

Introduction

Queen Victoria's ascension to the throne was a welcome relief after years of royalty who instilled neither pride nor admiration in the minds of their British subjects. She was young, pretty, and mindful of her duty to the country.

Queen Victoria's subjects watched with awe and admiration as she ascended to the throne, married, and gave birth to nine children. Victoria and her family were indeed royals in which to take pride.

As you might imagine, everything the royal family did, said, and wore became news. Because her subjects loved her, they tried to emulate her as much as possible. Consequently everything she wore became an instant fashion.

Victoria had such a tremendous impact on the world in which she lived that the very era bears her name. The most common of household items, be it a teacup, clock, or piece of furniture from her years on the throne, is now referred to as "Victorian."

Following this pattern, I titled this book *Collecting Victorian Jewelry*, even though it does not focus entirely on British jewelry from this time period. As you will see, jewelry in America and France is also featured. In fact, we highlight the American Civil War era in clothing fashions and jewelry to satisfy the ever-growing interest in the re-enactment of those years.

The years from 1837-1901 were some of the most progressive in history. Queen Victoria's reign saw the evolution of the horse-drawn carriage to the horseless carriage; the outdoor privy to the indoor toilet; and candlelight to electric lights. Railroads crisscrossed the country, and the industrial revolution introduced factories as a way of life.

Collecting Victorian Jewelry highlights world events during this era and how they influenced fashions in clothing and jewelry. Each decade is embellished with colored fashion plates from popular magazines of the day, such as *Graham's, Godey's Lady's Book*, and *Peterson's Magazine*. We take a decade-by-decade look at how these fashions in clothing had a direct influence on the jewelry of the time, and how newly discovered materials and new improvements in machinery affected how these pieces were made. This information is augmented by hundreds of color photographs of the jewelry, complete with prices from all ranges of the marketplace.

I take great pleasure in inviting you to join me in this adventure through these exciting years. Enjoy!

C. Jeanenne Bell

SECTION I

1806-1839 TIMELINE

1806—Berlin iron jewelry made in Germany.

1806-1814—French excavations of Pompeii.

1819—Victoria born on May 24 at Kensington Palace.

1820—George IV becomes king of England.

1825—National Academy of Arts and Design is established in America.

1820-1830s—"Regard" rings and brooches are popular acrostic jewelry.

1825-1850—Ferronier-style chain becomes popular.

1829—Andrew Jackson elected president of the United States.

1829—Anne of Geierstein published in 1829.

1830—William IV becomes king of England upon the death of George IV.

1830-1850s—Acrostic or "name" or "regard" rings are popular.

1830-1840s—"Shirt pins had short stems"; later (1850-1860), "stems longer and scored or twisted part way up to keep them from slipping out of the fabric."

1834—Fire destroys the old Royal Palace of Westminster.

1837—Queen Victoria ascends to the British throne. Romanticism and rococo styles are revived.

1837—Fiftieth anniversary of American independence.

1839—The Frenchman Louis-Jacques-Mandé Daguerre developed the daguerreotype.

The Beginnings
1819-1930s

The story of the Victorian era begins before Queen Victoria's birth in May 1819. About 1818, the Duke of Kent, who was destined to be the father of the queen of England, was persuaded by his trusted advisors to begin searching for a suitable wife. The need to provide an heir, plus the motivation of the extra allowance that he would receive as a married man, were the strong incentives needed to persuade him to put aside his longtime mistress.

On the ruse that he needed a letter delivered to his sister, Prince Leopold of Saxe Coburg, the brother-in-law of the duke, asked the duke to deliver a letter to his sister in Germany. With this delivery the duke found his "proper" wife. She was Victoria Mary Louise, the princess of Leininges, a widow with two children who lived in a castle at Amorbach, Bavaria. The duke's smile, kind manner, and reputation as the "kind and popular" duke quickly won her heart and hand.

The marriage took place in Coburg on May 29, 1818, with the rites of the Lutheran Church. They remarried in England with a private ceremony at Krew Palace. Finances dictated that they make their home in Bavaria. When it became evident that the duchess was with child, the duke felt an urgency for his heir to be born on English soil. Consequently, in the last trimester of her confinement, they made the long, arduous trip to England.

There the future sovereign was born in Kensington Palace at 4:00 a.m. on May 24, 1819. She was named Alexandrina Victoria. When she was only two years old, her father died from pneumonia while they were in Devonshire near the sea. It was a cold January day in 1820 when her mother wisely chose to raise the child in England.

Kensington Palace where Queen Victoria was born.

This was a brave decision in light of the fact that she spoke only German and was in a country that was foreign

The Duchess of Kent is wearing a head ornament with a central jewel that hangs on her forehead. This type of jewelry was popular throughout the 1830s and 1840s. It was called a "ferronniere" and was based on a portrait from the 15th century of a lady thought to be a blacksmith's wife. The 19th century modified the piece with a chain instead of a ribbon. There were later versions of the style, which included a drop on each side of the central pendant. The duchess was said to have given Victoria three ferronnieres, each set with different types of stones for her 14th birthday.

to her. To complicate matters, she was not liked by her dead husband's relatives—one of whom just happened to be the king of England. In spite of these liabilities, she was determined to stay. She strongly believed in the words of a fortune teller that she had visited while pregnant with Victoria. The prediction that "the child she was carrying would someday rule a great nation" was a strong incentive to stay.

It's hard to believe that anyone born in a palace to a member of the royal family could be considered a poor relation. But all things being relative, this was the case with Victoria and her mother. The £6,000 jointure given to them by William IV, Victoria's "Uncle King," was graciously supplemented by her Uncle Leopold. He acted as her guardian, and she always held him in the highest esteem. Even with his support, they led a frugal existence for royalty, especially for one who would one day be queen. Later, Leopold succeeded to the throne of Belgium. Victoria was blessed with many royal relatives.

As a child, Victoria had a very sheltered childhood. Her mother, being fearful of her enemies in "high places," never wanted Victoria out of her sight. In fact, she and Victoria slept in the same room. The idea that Victoria would someday be queen was always harbored in her mother's heart.

Little Victoria never had any playmates. She did have her older stepsister, Princess Feodore, who was eleven years her senior, but later she moved back to Germany. Instead, Victoria's days were filled with planned activities. Her lessons included English, German, French, and Latin. She also learned to ride horseback, draw, paint, and play the piano. Victoria was a happy child with a quick mind and a will of her own.

Before we start feeling too sorry for this poor little princess, we must remember that she had a loving mother, a nanny, tutors for all of her subjects, a carriage and donkey, many toys, approximately 200 dolls, and dinners with her "Uncle King." She wasn't poor in the sense that we consider poor, but she certainly wasn't exposed to many children her age, and she certainly didn't live the luxurious life of most royals.

Victoria at four years of age.

When she was twelve years old, it was first mentioned to her that she was in line to be the possible queen of England. There are various stories about exactly how and by whom this information was delivered to her, but suffice it to say she was mature enough to understand the seriousness of her position. After this time, she was included in many more court activities.

Her first recorded encounter with the young man who was destined to be her "beloved Albert" was in May 1836, when she was seventeen years old. Her Uncle Leopold arranged the visit of her cousins Ernest and Albert to Kensington Palace. Victoria and Albert shared the same German grandmother so they had many things in common. She enjoyed the young men's visit and looked forward to another one in the future.

Queen Victoria

In the predawn hours of June 20, 1837, eighteen-year-old Victoria was awakened to be informed by Lord Archbishop Howle and Chamberlain Lord Conyengham that her uncle, the king of England, had died. She was now the queen of England. When she was informed of her new status, she was said to have vowed, "I will be good." And she was good, so good that the era bears her name. Today every item made during her reign, whether it is a teacup, clock, or even jewelry, is identified as Victorian.

Her coronation was held in Westminster Abbey on Thursday, June 28. Literally speaking, the old crown was too heavy on her head. It weighed more than seven pounds. Consequently, she had commissioned a new, daintier one that was extremely elegant and, just as important, weighed only three pounds. The stones in the new crown were taken from the crown that had been worn by George IV and William IV.

Rev. John Rusk, Ph.D., describes the street scenes on Coronation Day in his book, *The Beautiful Life and Illustrious Reign of Queen Victoria:*

London was awake very early on that day, and by 6 o'clock strings of vehicles poured into the West End. Crowds of foot-passengers also were on the move, all converging towards one point. From Hyde Park Corner to the Abbey there was scarcely a house without a scaffolding, soon to be filled with sightseers. Seats were sold at a very high rate, while tickets at more than twenty guineas each; and the Earl Marshal had to apprise the public that forged tickets were in circulation, the holders of which would not only be stopped but given into custody. Not withstanding the immense number of persons in the Gren Park and St. James' Park, and in the vicinity of Buckingham Palace, the police and military preserved admirable order.

At 10 o'clock a salute of twenty-one guns and the hoisting of the imperial standard in front of the palace, intimated that Her Majesty had entered the state carriage. The procession then set forth, preceded by trumpeters and a detachment of Life Guards. Then came the foreign Ministers and Ambassadors, followed by the carriages of the royal family. Her Majesty appeared in excellent spirits, and highly delighted with the imposing scene. The troops saluted in succession as she passed, and remained with presented arms until the royal carriage had passed the front of each battalion, the bands continuing to play the National Anthem. It is said that every window along the route was a bouquet, every balcony a parterre of living loveliness and beauty; and as the queen passed, scarfs, handkerchiefs and flowers were waved with the most boisterous enthusiasm. Her Majesty was more than once visibly affected by these exhilarating demonstrations, and occasionally turned to the Duchess of Sutherland to conceal or express her emotion.

The ceremony continued with only a few small things going wrong in the formal proceedings. The most painful incident in the ceremony happened during the investiture of the ring and the scepter. A ruby ring was supposed to be placed on her ring finger. Unfortunately, the ring had been sized to go on her pinkie instead. She offered her little finger to the archbishop, but he insisted that it must be placed on the fourth finger. After she removed her other rings, it was forced on to the "proper" finger. As soon after the ceremony as possible, she soaked her finger in ice water and removed the painful ring.

Queen Victoria at the time of her accession.

Finally, Victoria was officially queen! One of the first things she had done after being notified of her new status was to order a room of her own. Never again would she have to share a room with her mother. She rather enjoyed her newfound freedom, but at the same time she understood the gravity of the tasks that lay ahead. Fortunately she was wise enough to surround herself with good advisors.

Queenly Gossip

Having a young queen was a delightful alternative to the old kings that had reigned before. It was only natural that everyone would be curious about the young new queen. Everything she did, said, and wore became newsworthy.

In February and March 1839, nine months after the coronation, *Godey's Lady's Book* had lengthy articles about the new queen. Even though the writer of the article begins by saying that people are probably tired of talking about the queen, he or she goes on about Queen Victoria page after page, so much so that they had to continue the article in the next issue. One of the writer's complaints were the stories about the queen that were deemed "newsworthy." Even though the writer was critical of this, it didn't stop her from telling them again. The following are only excerpts from these lengthy articles.

It may seem to some of my readers a late hour for an article on the Queen. Most people are done talking and writing of her, I know. The universal enthusiasm which her accession excited, and which was for some time kept alive by many interesting circumstances following in the train of that event, has now in a great measure subsided, as well on the other side of the Atlantic as on this. The constant loyalty with which old John Bull has long been his Sovereign, noisy and warm as it usually is, was in this instance heightened by considerations almost peculiar to the case of Victoria; by her sex, her youth, her unsullied and unsuspected character, her maiden charms: and yet that generous glow of emotion already exists no more.

The Queen and the Mackintosh. While her Majesty was riding on horseback on Monday, in last week,

in Windsor Great Park, she and her party were surprised by a heavy shower of rain when they were yet at some little distance from the castle. A gentleman of her suite offered her Majesty his Mackintosh as a protection against the elementary attack. This her Majesty, with the most becoming condescension, instantly accepted and wore all the way home.

The strongest feeling of personal regard subsists between her Majesty and the Queen Dowager an instance of which, though slight in itself we are enabled to give. It is known that Queen Adelaide is passionately fond of flowers; and last year during her residence at Windsor, she planted some violets of a particular kind in those beautiful gardens near the castle, called the Slopes. It was only during her Majesty's late visit to Windsor, during Easter, that the violets bloomed for the first time this year, and as soon as her Majesty was informed of it, she immediately caused a bouquet to be gathered, and sent it off by express to Marlborough House, in order that Queen Adelaide might receive the first offering of the flowers which she herself had planted.

On the same principle, when her Majesty went to Guildhall to dine with the worshipful authorities of the City of London, it was formally announced with all the particulars, that having had the misfortune to throw down a China fire-screen in one of the relieving-rooms provided for her on that occasion, she absolutely turned round at the crash made by the fall; and, what is more marvelous still, if possible, opened her own mouth and said, "Oh dear! What a pity! What a beautiful screen!" Such were the phenomena, concerning the Queen, which the kingdom was treated with daily by the leading journals for months. They knew very well too, the taste which they catered for. They crowded their goods to a market. Everything of the sort which was set before him, old John devoutly gave thanks for, and consumed with an inconceivable relish. A paragraph of such gossip was as good as a pint of porter. An opportunity to stare and shout after the poor little lady, as she went out to ride, really helped his digestion. What must have been the emotions excited by the appearance of the following item: "The Queen has been graciously pleased to honor Madame Le Plastna, of 17, William street, Strand, with the appointment of "Stay and Corset Maker to her Majesty!"

At Kensington I used to hear, among people not so given to gossip, a story about the "gentleman who holds the stirrup," mentioned above. It was somebody of some merit and claims—needy and modest withal—an old acquaintance probably, who might have thought himself forgotten. Victoria, however, does not forget such things, neither does she overlook little things: she thinks nothing little, indeed, where the heart is concerned. The question arose what could be done for this worthy? There was no place he was fit for, everybody said. They thought it a pity—but so it was. "The offices all full" asked the Queen, tapping her impatient little foot on the carpet. "All full, your Majesty!" answered my lord. "Well, then, I must violate the constitution. I'll make an office. Make him my Stirrup-holder. Give him two hundred a year." No doubt worse appointments than this have been issued since the accession.

With a temperament of this kind, we can appreciate again, the pleasure the Queen must have had in the affectionate demonstrations of her people, and the effect it may be expected to have on her mind. A well informed Scotch writer, speaking on this head, states that her medical attendant, in whose charge she has been from her infancy, expressed to her Majesty a fear that she was exposed to too much excitement, and it might be injurious to her health. "Dismiss your fears, my dear doctor," was her reply; "you use a wrong expression. I know not what may come, but I have as yet met with so much affection, so much respect, and every act of sovereignty has been made so light, that I have not yet felt the weight of the crown." The doctor at the same time remarked upon her constant daily public dinners. "Oh," she exclaimed, "if I had a small party, I should then be called upon to exert myself to entertain my guests; but, with a large party, they are called upon to amuse me, and then I become personally acquainted with those who are to surround the throne."

She sleeps on a little mattress, which even Dr. Alcott might not object to. She rises early. A strict punctuality not only governs her own movements, but she contrives to see that all concerned with her observe this virtue as well. Something of this regularity, and of her good system of business habits in general, she may probably owe to the influence of the example of one of her favorites, the Duke of Wellington, one of the most consummate business characters in the world. It need not be hinted how important these habits are in the Queen's situation. As Queen, she has really a good many indispensable engagements—a great deal of drudgery included. Her signature, for example, must be given to a vast variety of documents—commissions for the army and navy, among the rest. She has probably commenced her reign with the general determination to take her full measure of all the legitimate responsibilities of her station. She has a conscience and an ambition both, on this point. If she does not discover the masculine salient energy of Elizabeth, as she is not likely, either to have desire or occasion to do, she will not have it said of her that she shrinks from the discharge of her real duty. She knows and feels that there is much for her to do, much to endure, at the best. This she has made up her mind bravely to take as it comes: and to this end, as well as for other reasons, she cultivates the health and hardihood of her whole constitution.

I have been often asked, how does the Queen look? Is she pretty? Is she handsome? This is a most momentous point to us Republicans, of course; so much so, and so delicate an affair moreover in itself—this description and discussion of a lady's countenance—nay, of a Queen's that I must even decline the task. The most I could depose would be, in general terms—"rather pretty!" I hope this is no profanation to say. The Queen, it is well known, is quite short—too much so for dignity; rather dumpy, as we call it—I beg pardon again; her form not remarkably ethereal—more of the substantial style which we might expect from her habits, as well as her lineage, and of which her friends, if not her admirers, will make no complaint. Her features partake a little open, almost showing the tip of the tongue. This is not very intellectual, but I cannot help that. The Duchess is said to object always to the painters representing it as it is, while Victoria herself is understood to insist on a strict likeness, and to succeed in having her own way. The best thing in the face, on the whole, is the expression. This is decidedly prepossessing—not imposing at all. It is sincere, frank, warm-hearted. On the strength of this, chiefly, I should describe her as "rather pretty," and I can conceive of its proving so much so, to those associate with her, or see her often, or under certain circumstances of excitement, as to make her pass for more than this. Hence I have heard her called even handsome. Some of my readers will better judge of this opinion when I say that she resembles Mrs. Smith, of the Tremont Theatre, more than any other lady I ever saw; and this remark has been made by others who know both.

The size and stature are very nearly the same; Mrs. Smith's features seem, however, more petite. Her face is less German. In action, also, she is much more brisk. The Queen's postures, gait, and general bearing, are as dignified perhaps, as her diminutive person will allow; of course there is nothing like alertness about her, on public occasions at least. It does very well for a rider to be spry, I suppose it will not do for a Queen!

Albert Returns

When Albert and Ernest returned in 1839, Victoria was surprised to see that Albert had lost his baby fat and had grown tall and even more handsome. Some say that she fell in love with him the instant that she saw him again. They spent time together playing duets on the piano and talking about Albert's many travels.

Her advisors were eager for her to marry and produce an heir to the throne. Prior to Albert's return visit, Victoria had been reluctant to think about giving up her newfound freedom. She had many suitors who came to call, but now her mind was set on Albert. Before he left she made her intentions known to him. As the Queen, it was up to her to propose to him. She did so with apologies for what he would have to give up to become her husband. She was aware of the circumstances in which the marriage would place him and the sacrifices that he would be called upon to make. In spite of this, he gladly accepted her proposal.

She notified her advisors and set up a time to announce her intentions to Parliament. Upon hearing of the engagement, they immediately passed a bill to naturalize Albert as a citizen of England. After some debate, they also granted him an annuity of £30,000. Albert set about to transfer his estate in Germany to his older brother.

Albert presented Victoria with an engagement ring of a serpent motif set with an emerald. The wedding was set for Feb. 10, 1840. Preparations began for the big occasion.

This book includes a brief look at these beginning years because fashions in clothing and jewelry evolve slowly, especially in the early years of the Victorian period. Some types of jewelry that were made in these years remained popular for many decades.

Fashions in the Early Years

By 1819 the Grecian neo-classical look, which was never popular for clothing in England, was becoming passé in France. The following excerpt from *The Designer* magazine from November 1898 offers comments on fashions of the 1820-1830s:

The caprices of Madame la Mode have so long furnished entertaining subject matter for this space-writer's ready pen that it were in no wise surprising if the comparative immunity from extravagance of the present style of costume plunged that ingenious and hardworking individual to the lowest abyss of professional despair. Yet, so many and diverse have been the sartorial absurdities of the past, that whole volumes might yet be written concerning them without exhausting the store of interesting data that history has handed down to us.

1820s-1830s

By the spring of 1820, the waistline had been restored to its normal position, and the corset, which for a decade or so had been practically out of count, resumed its usual functions. What ensued may well be termed the era of the décolleté, for gowns of all kinds, whether designed for indoor or outdoor wear, were cut with low bodices and short, puffed sleeves that generally extended not more than half-way to the elbow. Sometimes another puff was added, reaching from the elbow to the wrists; but the ultra fashionable mundane usually preferred to expose her shapely arms, simply adding to her toilette a pair of lace-topped gloves. Large-brimmed hats, much bedecked with bows and feathers, were also a conspicuous feature of the 1820 mode, as was the quaint little "spencer," or shoulder cape, which the low-cut gowns rendered quite indispensable to delicate feminine chests, and the dainty sandaled slippers, which displayed "my lady's slender feet," as immortalized by Sir John Suckling, to the best possible advantage.

In the fifteen years between 1820 and 1835, broad shoulders, immense sleeves, and bell skirts were in vogue, giving way in the course of time to the sloping shoulders and full skirts illustrated on the first figure on this page. Simultaneously, the "Restoration" or "Marie Amélie" bonnet appeared, named in honor of the consort of Louis XVIII, for the ill-fated House of Orleans had temporarily been restored to its own. This quaint headpiece, with its broad, poke brim, jam-pot crown and jaunty tie-strings, was even more becoming to a fair, youthful face than the enormous hat that it superseded; in fact, its apparent innocent demureness was in reality nothing more or less than a snare for the hearts of susceptible masculinity. Yet, when a futile attempt was made some four or five years later to restore it to favor, it was almost unanimously voted hideously unbecoming, and the modern belle would have none of it!

The Jewelry
Cannetille

A shortage of gold instigated a new style of metalwork in the 1820s. Once again the pendulum had swung in the opposite direction, and instead of sections of jewelry being flat and two-dimensional, they were now raised in a metalwork design known as cannetille. This French word for embroidery aptly describes the fine workmanship. The building up of fine gold threads gave a bulky, heavy look to a very lightweight piece of jewelry. Eventually the English were able to make molds and cast look-alike cannetille. By close inspection one can learn to tell the difference.

Close-up of cannetille work in a piece of jewelry.

Stones

Topaz, amethyst, garnets, and citrines were very popular stones in this time period. But no matter what the stone, it's safe to assume that its color was enhanced by foil if it had a closed backing. The foiling of stones not only helped enhance the color, but it was a godsend to the jeweler who was trying to match stones for a piece.

Jewelry with an unusual assortment of stones that holds a message is known as acrostic. The stones in this type of jewelry are arranged so that the first letter of the name of each stone spells a word. For instance, the stones arranged in the heart drop shown in the accompanying picture spell out the word "regard." The top left stone is a ruby, followed by an emerald, garnet, amethyst (in which the color is distorted by a light in the center of the stone), and another ruby, with a diamond set in the center. The giver is not only sending his heart but also his sentiments.

The "Regard" heart drop is an example of acrostic jewelry.

Bloodstone

Bloodstone can be found in jewelry made throughout the Victorian era. Although it is seldom used today, the Victorians wore and admired it. This ancient stone, also known as heliotrope (hee-lee-trope), is actually a dark green chalcedony with flecks of red. The ancients believed the flecks of red to be drops of blood, hence the name "bloodstone." Many magical powers were ascribed to it, including the power to stop bleeding and preserve health. Bloodstone is one of the birthstones for March. When a piece of jewelry contains bloodstone, it is usually old.

A piece of uncut bloodstone.

Turquoise

The word "turquoise" originates from the words meaning Turkish stone. Because turquoise came to Europe en route from Turkey, people mistakenly thought that was where the stone was mined.

The Victorians loved turquoise and wore it in jewelry throughout the century. It was especially favored by young girls because it was beautiful to wear (diamonds were considered a stone worn by matrons). But it was by no means limited to this age group. The soft unlined blue turquoise color complemented so many faces that both young and old wore it. The preferred color was sky blue, which is usually associated with Persian turquoise. Victorians never used the turquoise webbed with matrix that we think of as "southwest."

This gold brooch is set with cabochon-cut garnets, amethysts, emeralds and turquoises. That may seem like a strange combination of stones today.

A closer view of turquoise stones. Notice that some of them have changed in color, and at least two look as if they have been replaced with glass. Can you tell which ones?

Turquoise is a very porous stone. Today it is often treated with artificial resin to keep it from absorbing body oils, cosmetics, and perspiration. Because the stones were left untreated in the Victorian era, one will sometimes encounter necklaces and rings with stones that do not match in color. Some of the stones have changed to a greenish color, while others remain unchanged.

Many pieces of Victorian jewelry are embellished with small cabochons or balls of what appear to be turquoise, but on closer examination they turn out to be glass.

Don't think that just because a piece of jewelry is gold and old that the stones in it are real. Even the Egyptians often used glass substitutes for genuine stones.

Marcasites

The stone known as marcasite is actually pyrite (PIE-rite), an iron sulfite. There is a mineral named marcasite, and, although it is similar in appearance, it is not suitable for jewelry. This case of mistaken identity is now commonly accepted.

Marcasites were fashionable substitutes for diamonds as early as the 1700s. Legend tells us that a popular marquise favored the stone that we now call marcasite. It became known as the "marque's set" and eventually became marcasite.

When pyrite is faceted, its luster is metallic, and the brilliance comes from light reflecting off the facets. Marcasites were always mounted in silver, as were the diamonds of the period. In the mid-1800s marcasites once again gained favor. Their reflective sparkles adorned pins, earrings, necklaces, bracelets, and buckles.

Genuine marcasites are usually set with metal holding the stones in place. On later inexpensive pieces they were often glued into cast mountings that gave the appearance of having beads holding them. It takes an examination with a loupe to make this determination because, although some pieces often have the small beads of metal that appear to be holding the stone, a closer look will reveal that the beads are not even touching the marcasite. The metal in which the stones were set and the design of the piece are factors that greatly influence price.

Marcasites were later imitated in plastic.

Irish necklace and bracelet with pyrite, or marcasites, set in silver. Sometimes the pyrite was set in little slabs instead of being faceted into what we know as marcasites.

Hold-Over Materials

The reason we start this book with pieces from many years before Victoria became queen is that so many materials that were used in other centuries were popular in the 1800s. Knowledge of stylistic designs and mountings will help in circa dating.

As you will see in future time periods, the Victorian era is known for its eclecticism. Victorians liberally borrowed styles from the Middle Ages through the 18th century. Popular motifs such as Gothic, renaissance, baroque, Louis XIV, rococo, and Louis XVI styles were lavishly mixed with other motifs, thereby making them uniquely Victorian. [1]

Not only were motifs borrowed from the past, but also materials used in earlier times continued to be popular. Let's explore some of these.

Berlin Iron

The hold-over material with the shortest span of popularity in the Victorian era was Berlin iron. It is often associated with the 1812-1814 time period, but it was actually popular into the 1850s.

Records indicate that the first iron jewelry was probably made in the Gleiwitz in Silesia. This factory produced all types of ironwork including bridges. Records also show that Berlin iron jewelry was made in France as early as 1798.[2] Iron jewelry probably evolved from the silhouette plaques of iron that the factory workers cast. By miniaturizing these plaques and medallions and joining them, they could be made to complement the popular styles of the day.

In 1804 the Royal Berlin Factory was opened. Located behind the grounds of Charité, it was known for its iron jewelry. It's from this factory that the name "Berlin iron" became associated with this type of jewelry.

This association is the most prevalent because in order to raise money for the war efforts, the patriotic residents of this city started exchanging their gold jewelry for iron pieces. The terms *"gold gab ich fur Eisen 1813"* (gold I gave for iron) and *"Ein git auschut zum wohl des Vanderlands"* (exchanged for the welfare for the fatherland) are sometimes, but certainly not always, cast or inscribed in these pieces. Sometimes pieces are signed, but according to Anne Clifford, author of the book *Cut-Steel and Berlin Iron Jewelry,* these are the manufacturers' names, not necessarily the names of the designers.

Berlin iron jewelry can be circa dated by the styles that were popular in a certain time period. For instance, the more classic designs that are backed with mother-of-pearl are associated with the years in which the neo-classic designs were popular. In 1834 Westminster Palace burned, and architect and designer Pugin used neo-Gothic motifs for the new palace of Westminster. His jewelry made in this design was a hit at the Crystal Palace exhibition in 1851. Berlin iron lent itself well to this neo-Gothic design and retained its popularity until the fashion for things Gothic went out of style.

Close-up of Silesian iron work. Note the cut-steel paillettes in the center of the medallion.

Many of the "sprung-wire" circles are associated with pieces made in Silesia, but they were also incorporated into pieces of Berlin iron jewelry. Most of the beautifully fine wirework was embellished with what was referred to as cut-steel paillettes, or sequins. Take a moment and look at the medallion in the accompanying picture and note the center embellishment with cut-steel.

It may sound surprising, but not all Berlin iron jewelry was made in Berlin. When Napoleon occupied the city, he took molds back to France. Consequently, some pieces were made there. Australian factories also made the jewelry. They obtained their models from Prussia, and the pieces were made in Bohemia.[3]

Berlin iron bracelet circa 1820-1830.

Berlin iron necklace, circa 1815-1820, with iron cameos on polished steel mountings.

It is not surprising that the supply of Berlin iron jewelry is limited, but the find is definitely worth the hunt. Many dealers admire and appreciate these pieces, but bargains are still to be found. Pieces currently have been offered at half (or less) of their market value. As usual, the knowledgeable buyer can find bargains.

Other than a full range of jewelry, there were other toys, as they were called, made of Berlin iron: trinket boxes, watch keys, and even tiny purses. I purchased one of these tiny bags for $20 from a dealer who didn't know or seem to care about what it was made of or where it was made. Her apathy was my good fortune.

Cut-Steel

Cut-steel is made by riveting rosettes fashioned from thin metal to another metal plate that has been cut in a design. Although it is called cut-steel, in less-expensive items the metal can be silver alloy or even tin. The glitter of cut-steel comes from light reflecting off the rosettes. Imitation cut-steel is made by stamping the rosettes from a sheet of metal. The best way to determine the authenticity of a piece is by looking at the back. If there are two pieces of metal and one is a solid plate with rivets showing, chances are that the piece is a genuine 19th century (or earlier) piece.

Cut-steel jewelry was popular almost a century before Victoria was born, but it continued to be very popular throughout the 1850s. This doesn't mean it was no longer made after this date because it certainly was. In fact, you can find it incorporated in jewelry as late as the 1930s.

The fascination with cut-steel began with its ability to glitter and reflect the light in a way that imitated the much more expensive diamond. What the steel jewelry lacked in an intrinsic value was compensated by the beautiful craftsmanship seen in many of the pieces.

Records indicate that the cut-steel industry flourished in the town of Woodstock, England, a few miles north of Oxford, as early as 1720. Woodstock's reputation for producing the finest quality pieces brought orders from as far away as Florence, Italy. By 1871 cut-steel items were also being made in Birmingham. In Anne Clifford's book, *Cut-Steel and Berlin Iron Jewelry,* she quotes Sylias Neville's comment about why Woodstock pieces were superior to those made in Birmingham: "Their watch-chains, sword hilts, etc. are more highly polished and better studded than those of Birmingham. They polish all their pieces with the hand. Then the studs, screws, and everything they make can be taken to pieces for cleaning where as the Birmingham studs are united."

Despite these discouraging words, Birmingham was still well known for its cut-steel industry. One noted producer in Birmingham was Matthew Boulton, who made beautiful rings and brooches using Wedgwood cameos set in cut-steel frames.

One of my favorite 19th century authors, Charles Dickens, gives this childhood viewpoint about cut-steel in his book, *David Copperfield.* Writing about his step-aunt's jewelry boxes, his young character says, "The two black boxes were never seen open or known to be unlocked and where (for I peeped in once or twice when she was out) numerous little steel fetters and rivets, with which Miss Murdstone embellished herself when she was dressed, generally hung upon the looking glass in a formidable array."

Cut-steel bracelet made in the garter motif.

The underside of the cut-steel bracelet.

The Victorian pieces should be constructed in the manner described earlier. Consequently, the only way to really date a piece of that type is by stylistic design and scale, which in itself can sometimes be a challenge. The author of *Victorian Jewellery*, Margaret Flower's clue for detecting the country of origin is that the French favored oval rosettes and the English favored round ones. One clue that I have used to help date a piece is by counting the number of facets on each "head." The 18th century pieces tend to have as many as 15 facets and the 19th century pieces have as few as five. Cut-steel jewelry can be very delightful, and it can make quite a beautiful and wearable collectible.

Pietre Dure

The mosaics from Florence, Italy are commonly known as "pietre dure," which literally means "hard stone." These works of art are made by cutting designs out of stones such as malachite, carnelian, and a variety of quartz. The pieces are fitted together to made a design in a black background. This is done so expertly that a magnifying glass is needed to verify that the design is indeed made from pieces and not painted. Flowers, birds, and butterflies are some of the favorite motifs. As you will see in the jewelry pictures throughout this book, these motifs were repeated over and over again.

Medici used this technique at his "Opificio delle Pietre Dure," which he founded in the 16th century. At that time, pietre dure was used to embellish furniture and panels. Many of the plaques that originally decorated fine furniture were recycled into brooches in the first quarter of the 19th century. Necklaces from the early 1800s were also taken apart, and the plaques were used for brooches later in the century. There are some lovely examples included in almost all of the time periods in this book.

Beautiful pietre dure inlay.

Roman Mosaics

As early as the early 18th century, the Vatican was making pieces of Roman mosaic jewelry to sell to visitors. The mosaics made in Rome have an entirely different look from those made in Florence. They are made of tiny glass bricks, or tesserae, fitted together to make a picture. Popular motifs are Roman scenes or architectural ruins.

These mosaics continued to be popular in the Victorian era. They filled a need for the growing number of tourists that mushroomed during these years. Many designs were taken from the mosaics unearthed in the ruins of Pompeii. They were especially popular with the visitors to that area.

Note the little rectangular glass tesserae in this Roman mosaic brooch.

A magnifying glass is needed to fully appreciate these tiny works of art. It is also recommended that you turn the piece so the light glances off the surface to make the tiny pieces more visible.

Seed Pearl Jewelry

Seed pearl jewelry is one of my favorite types of jewelry. One reason for my fascination is that someone actually drilled holes in these tiny things without breaking them. Another reason is that they were sewn onto a mother-of-pearl background with white horsehair. The result of all these efforts is usually a beautiful, delicate-looking piece of jewelry that is, in my opinion, fit for a queen.

When I first started studying antique jewelry over 35 years ago, I believed that this beautiful jewelry was only made in the 18th and early 19th centuries. Now I know that it was made throughout almost the entire 19th century. I even have one jewelry catalog from the second decade of the 20th century that includes some seed pearl earrings. My theory is that this must have been some Victorian "old store stock" that had been discovered and easily converted to the screw-type backs, which were popular during that time period. The seed pearls were only in one catalog, and the next edition of that catalog did not include them. That's one of the fun things about antique jewelry: There are always mysteries to solve.

Usually the open-worked two-dimensional pieces are older.

Seed pearl necklace, circa 1815.

As the clothes became fuller and heavier, jewelry pieces became fuller with less space in between pearls and sections. Even though the manufacturing process changed very little, the style and scale of the pieces changed.

In the 1860s metal supports such as the ones shown in this photo were added to larger delicate pieces of jewelry.

Pique

Pique is another material that was popular for well over a hundred years before the Victorians revived it. It has been in and out of fashion as far back as the 16th century. In the 18th century it was a popular material for watchcases. The Victorians loved it because, not only were the pieces tiny works of art, but the lightweight material could be made into large-scale pieces of jewelry to complement the fashion of the day without weighing down ears or dresses.

The popular French definition of the word pique is "dotted" or "cracked." This is an apt description of the beautiful work done in tortoiseshell or ivory. The most frequently encountered pique is done in tortoiseshell, which comes from the hawkbill turtle. Even though this is the smallest of marine turtles, it usually weighs between 100 and 200 pounds. Both the mottled upper shell and the lower "yellow belly" are used for ornamental purposes.

Tortoiseshell is one of nature's natural plastics. It can be heated and molded or cut into many forms. For pique, the shell is heated and a design is formed (star, cross, etc.). "Dots" or "racks" are drilled into this design. These minute spaces are inlaid with silver or gold rods. The hot tortoiseshell emits a glue-like film, which, along with the natural contraction caused by the cooling shell, snugly seals the metal.

Tortoiseshell pique bracelet.

Tortoiseshell jewelry remained popular throughout the century. Because it was a lightweight material, it could be made into large pieces when the fashion demanded, but it also lent itself well to the smaller, more delicate fashions near the end of the century. Unfortunately, during the 1870s, machines started to be used in the manufacturing process. As a result, the patterns became more geometric and the artistry was not as good as it was when the pieces were hand-cut.

Cameos

Cameos are made by cutting away background material to make a design in relief. In stone cameos, a banded agate is often used. The lighter band is used for the figure of the cameo. The remainder is carved away to expose the darker ground. For both shell and stone cameos, the true artist takes advantage of different layers and faults in the material to enhance the design.

Napoleon contributed to the desirability and appreciation of cameos. His excavations awakened interest in this old art. When he made Josephine a parure of ancient cameos, they became a new instant fashion statement. In 1805 Napoleon the first initiated a Prix de Rome to encourage stone engraving. About that same time, a public school was opened in Rome for the study of cameo engraving. Founded by Pope Leo XII, it met with much success.

Throughout the century, people studied, collected, and wore cameos set in all types of jewelry and accessories. Everything from tiaras to watch fobs were set with these beautiful little works of art. For those who couldn't afford authentic cameos, plaster casts of the ancient ones were sold complete with multi-drawer cabinets. These were used to study the beautiful artwork and the mythological tales they often conveyed. This became a common drawing room pastime. It was one of the few entertainments acceptable for a Sunday afternoon.

Originally cameos were carved from stone. Amethyst, garnet, citrine, onyx, agate, sardonyx, carnelian, coral, lava, and jet were all popular. The demand for lower-priced cameos brought about the use of readily available and, most of the time, free shells. Carvers used black helmet shells and the pink and white queen's conches, which were plentiful in the seacoast towns of Italy.

Cameos made lovely, portable souvenirs for tourists visiting the ruins of Pompeii and Herculaneum. When the travelers returned home, their friends were enchanted with these small works of art. Within a short time, Italian cameo artists had shops in England, France, and America. These craftsmen carved cameos in the ancient styles or any other designs the purchaser might select. The January 1850 issue of *Godey's Lady's Book* included the following note: "Peabody the celebrated Cameo Portrait Cutter, 140 Chestnut Street, is kept busily engaged with the portraits of some of our most eminent citizens."

The artist who created this Victorian cameo made use of four layers of the stone. This is a sign of good workmanship.

Queen Victoria, who was adept at art and sketching, took cameo-carving lessons. Cameos were popular throughout the Victorian period. Unfortunately, as the century progressed, the art of cameo carving declined. The majority of cameos being carved for today's tourists in Rome are generally of poor quality. Many exhibit sharp lines and poor workmanship. To find an artistry-carved cameo, the connoisseur must visit the small towns on the southern coast of Italy or, better yet, visit your favorite antiques shop.

Ivory

Ivory has been carved and worked since prehistoric times. Almost every age has treasured it, but prices for ivory reached an all-time high in the Victorian era. During this time period, there were several major ivory industries that were supplying jewelry to the trade. These included Paris and Dieppe, France, Naples, Italy, and Erbach, Germany.

The oldest ivory industry was located in the picturesque town of Dieppe, France, which has been a major ivory carving center for over 300 years. Known for its fine craftsmanship, the city has created model ships, statues, and church pieces. The ivory was brought into the harbor by sailors on their way back from Africa.

It was not until the 19th century that Dieppe turned its talents to carving jewelry. It could have been because of the tourist trade made possible by the fact that in the 1820s the city became the first seaside resort in France. Much of Dieppe's ivory jewelry was exported to nearby England.

Another town known for its ivory pieces was Erbach, Germany. The curator of the museum in Dieppe stated that before Count Franz von Erbach established his school and workshop in 1781, he visited the workshops in Dieppe to learn more about their methods.

The Erbach workshop became famous for its brooches with "stag and deer in the forest" motifs. Of course, when one workshop's designs became popular, the other workshops soon produced the same designs. Friedrich Hartmann from the Erbach workshop is said to have come up with the design containing a spray of roses in a beautiful hand, known as the "Erbacherf Rosen." [4]

Jewelry made of ivory was popular throughout the Victorian years. It was shown at all the major exhibitions during the 19th century. Because all the workshops made the same designs, it is difficult to determine exactly where a piece was made, unless the history of the ownership of the piece can be traced to a particular place.

When I visited Dieppe early in 2004, there were only two ivory carvers left in the city. One man, who at 53 years old is a master craftsman, has a shop on the corner of a narrow street. He does beautiful work and also has a good collection of antique ivory carvings. If you ever get to this picturesque town, be sure to visit his studio. The other carver in the town is located just down the street from the first and is 83 years old. He still carves in the tradition of his grandfather, who started there in 1840. The main problem for these two wonderful craftsmen is finding material to work. They usually resort to recycling old broken pieces. Consequently, their carvings are usually small.

A beautiful example of the Erbach rose.

The two museums in the town have wonderful examples of ivory carving covering a 300-year span. One is housed in a castle built in the 15th century. Situated on a hill, the Chateau Mesee De Dieppe also offers a great view of the city. The other museum is the Cite de La mer Mer de Dieppe and is located downtown. Be sure to take the time to visit both.

The best place to buy ivory jewelry (other than Dieppe) is in the United States. Because of the bad publicity about elephant poachers, the market is down and the prices are low.

An ivory carver from a painting in the Chateau-Musee De Dieppe.

This cherub with wings was carved by an 83-year-old carver in Dieppe, France.

Hold-Over Motifs

Some motifs were popular throughout the 19th century. Serpent or snake motifs and garter motifs are the two that most readily come to mind. They occurred over and over again in different materials and scale. Let's take a closer look at the serpent.

Snake or Serpent Motifs

When Albert presented Victoria with her engagement ring, it was designed as a snake with an emerald-set head. If a man of today did this, the woman would probably wonder if he could not afford a diamond.

DeBeers and its advertising agency, AW Ayers, are responsible for the diamond becoming the symbol of "forever." This idea was sold to the public all through the 20th century, and today buyers assume that diamonds are the correct stone for an engagement ring.

Albert could afford to give his intended any type of ring, but in those years the snake was a symbol of eternal love, and the queen was particularity fond of this design. The emerald was Victoria's birthstone, and it was popular in those days to have one's birthstone set in the engagement ring.

The snake motif was used throughout the Victorian period. On a stroll through London, ladies could be seen wearing serpent rings, serpents entwined around their arms, and serpents coiled on their brooches.

Memorial brooch in 18k gold and woven hair. The snake has ruby eyes with a garnet drop pendant in its mouth. The stone is closed back and engraved with the deceased's name and death in 1839.

In the book *David Copperfield* by Charles Dickens, published in 1850, a character tells of window shopping with his wife: "We look into the glittering windows of the jeweler's shops and I show Sophy which of the diamond-eyed serpents, coiled up on white satin rising-grounds, I would give her if I could afford it."

The snake motif remained popular throughout the entire century for bracelets, rings, earrings, and necklaces. It remained a symbol of love until the end of the century, when it was sometimes depicted as a sinister predator.

Serpent necklace and armlet, English, circa 1835-1840, set in silver and gold with pavé-set turquoises, rubies, pearls, and diamonds.

Metals

Pinchbeck

Pinchbeck is a metal with which most dealers and collectors of antique jewelry are familiar. What most of them do not know is that the man who invented it and for whom it was named was the famous watch and clock maker Christopher Pinchbeck (1670-1732). In fact, he was also the inventor of "Astronomico-Musical Clocks." He had a shop in London where he made and sold watches, clocks, and a variety of other items, including jewelry.

The metal he discovered contained no gold, but it looked like gold and wore well. It is not a plate or coating, but a solid metal, made (some say) by mixing four parts of copper and three parts zinc. The actual pinchbeck formula was a guarded secret passed down in the family, but other countries developed their own versions. There were so many imitations that Christopher Pinchbeck's grandson, Edward Pinchbeck, found it necessary to place this advertisement in the July 11, 1733 edition of the London *Daily Post*:

> *To prevent for the future the gross imposition that is daily put upon the public by a great number of Shop-Keepers, Hawkers, and Peddlers, in and about this town. Notice is hereby given that the ingenious Mr. Edward Pinchbeck, at the "Musical Clock" on Fleet Street, does not dispose of one grain of his curious metal, which so nearly resembles Gold in Color, Smell and Ductility, to any person whatsoever, nor are the Toys (watches, jewelry and trinkets) made of the said metal sold by any one person in England except himself; therefore gentlemen are desired to beware of imposters, who frequent Coffee Houses, and expose for sale, Toys pretended to be made of this metal, which is a most notorious imposition, upon the public.*

The following advertisement referred to necessary items for travel. Often copies of favorite pieces of jewelry were made to wear on travels. The gold ones were left safely at home. McKeever Persival, in his book Chats on Old Jewelry, states:

"In those days when a journey of even a few miles out of London led through roads infested by thieves and highway robbers, careful folk preferred not to tempt the 'gentlemen of the road' by wearing expensive ornaments unless traveling with a good escort; so not only would a traveler with a base metal watch and buckles lose less if robbed, by owing to the freemasonry which existed between innkeepers and pestilence and the highwaymen, they were actually less likely to be stopped, as it was not worth while to run risks for such a poor spoil."

With the invention of the electro-gilding process in 1840, and the legalization of 9k gold in 1854, the use of pinchbeck declined and eventually became passé. When antiquing in England, beware: The dealers there often refer to anything that is not solid gold as pinchbeck when actually it may be gold-filled or gold-plated. It is not the same.

Pinchbeck fob set with agate. This one has never been carved. It is pictured in its actual size.

The Fashions

Here are some fashions taken from women's magazines of the era. *Graham's Magazine, Peterson's Magazine,* and *Godey's Lady's Book* were popular magazines throughout the 19th century. These fashion plates were hand colored and continued to be so throughout the 1880s. Then we will visually explore the jewelry that was used to accessorize these fashions.

Godey's Lady's Book *fashion plate for May 1839.*

Godey's Lady's Book *summer 1839.*

Godey's *fashions for December 1839. This one also includes the latest in drapery styles.*

Pricing Section
1819-1830s

Bracelets

Photo courtesy Sotheby's of London 12-16-03 (A)

Photo of snake included in the lot.

Gold enamel and seed pearl serpent hinged bangle and ring, circa 1845, set with royal blue enamel and seed pearls, the eyes with cabochon garnets and with engraved floral and foliate decoration, diameter approximately 50 mm.

Price: $1,944

John Joseph (D)

Back view showing mesh-like chain and underside of stone.

Bracelet, circa 1820-'30s, cannetille work and amethyst stones.

Price: $3,150

Close-up of enamel work.

Close-up of watch.

Sharen Duncan-August (D)

Bracelet watch, circa 1830s, Swiss enamel with diamonds, rubies, and emeralds embellishing the case and bracelet; attached ring is worn on the finger to secure the watch on the top of the wrist; movement by Le Roi.

Price: $12,000

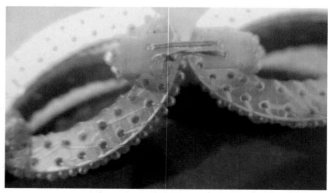

Jane Fletcher (D)

18k bracelet, circa 1840s, made with seed pearls.

Price: $750

Back view of two links showing that the pearls are backed with mother of pearl and attached by white horsehair.

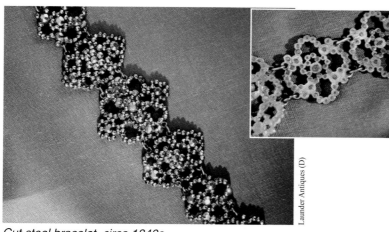

The back view shows how the beads were put on individually.

Launder Antiques (D)

Cut steel bracelet, circa 1840s.

Price: $455

Brooches

Launder Antiques (D)

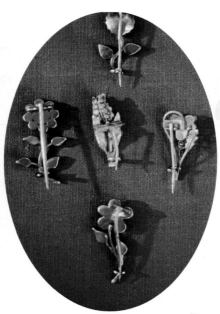

This back view shows the tube hinge, c-clasp, long pin stem, and closed backs. Closed backs usually have foiled stones to enhance their color when needed.

Five flower brooches, all circa 1820. They are called lace pins because they were scattered in lace collars. The top one has garnets and seed pearls; the one in the middle row, left side, is coral with hair in the center; the one in the middle is a tulip motif set with turquoise; the middle row right brooch is set with pink topaz; and the bottom brooch is an amethyst flower centered with a pearl. These are excellent examples of the types of stones used in this period. The small scale might be confused with pieces from the 1890- 1910 time period, but a look at the back will show the difference.

Price: $800

Veritas (D)

Brooch, circa 1820s, citrine and emeralds in beautiful cannetille worked gold.

Price: $750

Sue Brown (D)

Brooch, circa 1815, French pique of tortoiseshell and gold.

Price: $1,341

John Joseph (D)

View of locket open, showing lock of hair.

Brooch/locket, circa 1820s, a love token with stones that spell out the word "REGARD," note the snake coiled around the edge of the brooch, measures 1-1/16" x 7/8".

Price: $5,310

Sharen Duncan-August (D)

Brooch, circa 1830s, mixed metal mounting with beautiful lava cameo.

Price: $750

Sharen Duncan-August (D)

Brooch, circa 1830s, 18k gold, carved scenic shell cameo, beautifully done.

Price: $1,500

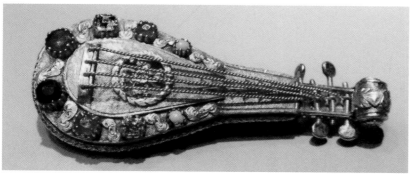

John Joseph (D)

Brooch, circa 1820s, mandolin-style brooch with stones flanked by turquoise, first letter of each stone forms the word "Regard," 2" x 7/8".
Price: $6,300, £3,500

Brooch with compartment open.

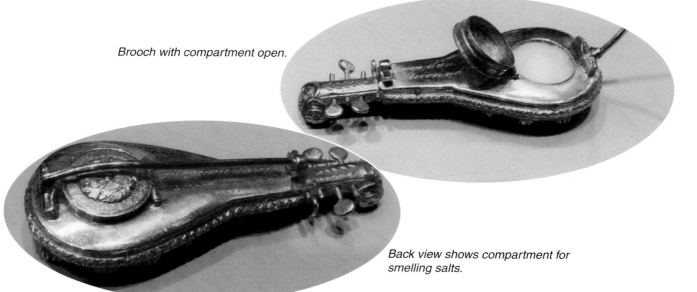

Back view shows compartment for smelling salts.

Earrings

Earrings, circa 1820s, turquoise with fine cannetille work.

Price: $675

Lauder Antiques (D)

Earrings, circa 1830s, pinchbeck, 3-1/2" x 4".

Price: $700

Sharen Duncan-August (D)

Sharen Duncan-August (D)

Earrings, circa 1830s, gold mounting set with amethyst.

Price: $600

Code by photograph credit line:

(A) Auction House—Auction Price

(C) Collector—Collector Asking Price

(D) Dealer—Dealer Asking Price

Necklaces

Bernard Cohen (D)

Necklace, circa 1820, Prussian iron cross and medallion with matching long guard chain, very rare, not many pieces have survived; medallion and cross are embellished with small pieces of cut steel.

Price: $3,600

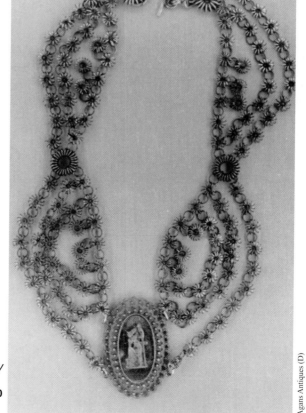

Close-up of medallion showing ironwork with cut steel center.

Necklace, Berlin iron, approximately 16" long.

Price: $1,500

Agans Antiques (D)

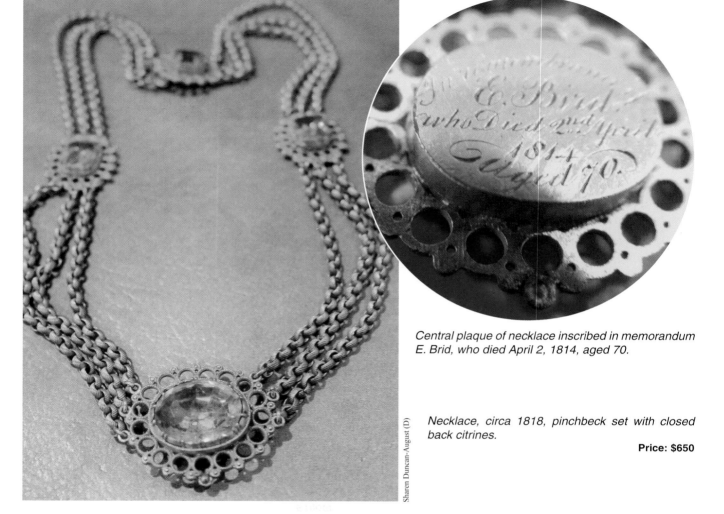

Central plaque of necklace inscribed in memorandum E. Brid, who died April 2, 1814, aged 70.

Necklace, circa 1818, pinchbeck set with closed back citrines.

Price: $650

Sharen Duncan-August (D)

Close-up of central cameo plaque.

Necklace, circa 1820-'30s, carved coral and turquoise with natural half pearls.

Price: $7,200

Sharen Duncan-August (D)

Necklace, circa 1820-'30s, flowers and stones set with agate drilled through with cut steel pinned in it, agates have mother of pearl backs.
Price: $900

Sharen Duncan-August (D)

Close-up of mammoth tooth material.

Necklace, circa 1840, mammoth tooth set in gilded metal.
Price: $450

Sharen Duncan-August (D)

Close-up of central plaque.

Necklace, circa 1820-'30s, Berlin iron necklace, 20" long, excellent condition with iron figures set on mother of pearl backs.
Price: $5,400, £3,000

Lauders Antiques (D)

Pendants

Lauder Antiques (D)

Pendant, circa 1820s, gold frame holding pietre dure of twin butterflies.

Price: $1,248, £695

Lauders Antiques (D)

Pendant, circa 1820s, gold mounting set with flat-cut garnets in the shape of pansies, closed back.

Price: $1,223, £680

> *Code by photograph credit line:*
>
> *(A) Auction House—Auction Price*
>
> *(C) Collector—Collector Asking Price*
>
> *(D) Dealer—Dealer Asking Price*

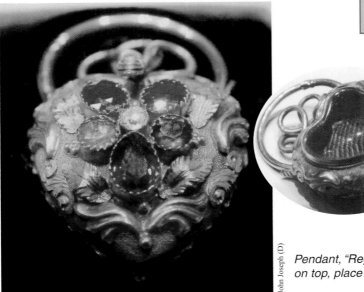

John Joseph (D)

Back view showing compartment for hair.

Pendant, "Regard" heart motif, circa 1820, snake on top, place in back for hair, 1-1/2" x 7/8".

Price: $7,020, £3,900

Pendant, circa 1820-'30s, pinchbeck locket.

Jeanenne Bell (C)

Price: $340

Locket open showing hair work, Prince of Well feather.

Rings

Sue Brown (D)

Ring, circa 1810, Regency carved stone cameo, carver started with three layers of colors.

Price: $3,960, £2,095

Photo courtesy Sotheby's of London
12-16-03 (A)

Hessonite garnet intaglio ring, early 19th century, the oval hessonite intaglio depicting a Greek kouros faces left, in a plain gold mount, ring size 0-1/2.

Price: $850-$1,200

Messada Antiques (D)

Ring, circa early 1800s, silver mounting with carved moonstone embellished with marcasites.

Price: $5,575, £2,950

View showing underside of head.

Messada Antiques (D)

Ring, circa 1820s, gold mounting with cushion cut flattop garnet.

Price: $1,087, £575

Code by photograph credit line:

(A) Auction House—Auction Price

(C) Collector—Collector Asking Price

(D) Dealer—Dealer Asking Price

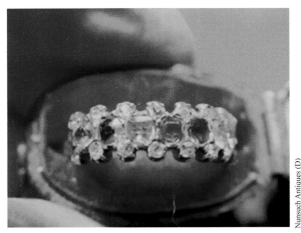

Nunsuch Antiques (D)

Ring, circa 1810, gold mounting set with diamond, amethyst, ruby, emerald, sapphire, and topaz, the first letter of each stone spells "Dearest."

Price: $1,444, £800

Jewelry Box Antiques (D)

Ring, circa 1820-'30s, 18k yellow gold, ruby, emerald, garnet, amethyst, ruby, and diamond, spells "Regard."

Price: $1,800

Sets

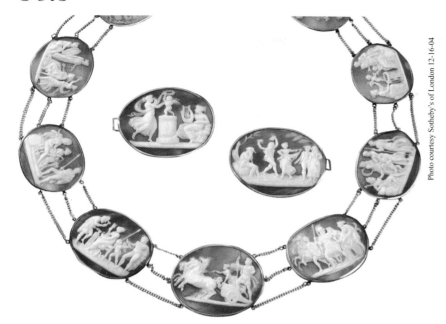

Photo courtesy Sotheby's of London 12-16-04

Shell cameo suite, circa 1800, comprised of a necklace, brooch, and a smaller plaque, the oval shell cameos depicting various mythological scenes, necklace length approximately 20 mm, bracelet length approximately 195 mm, brooch with later fitting.

Price: $8,640, £4,800

Jane Fletcher (D)

Close-up showing cannetille work in which the stones are set.

Necklace and earrings, circa 1820s, 18k gold set with rubies and emeralds, in original box, cannetille work.

Price: $2,200

Sharen Duncan-August (D)

Necklace and earrings, circa 1820s, pink topaz, aquamarine, rose-cut diamonds, and rubies around the flower (all foiled stones), remove pendant to make a brooch.

Price: $11,000, £6,100

Close-up of cannetille work. Look closely at the flower and notice the fine gold swirls that looks like embroidery thread from which the name "cannetille" is derived.

Back view of brooch with closed backs on stones.

Rams head mark on clasp.

Sharen Duncan-August (D)

Necklace, earrings, brooch, small scarf brooch and bracelet, circa 1830s, lava, bracelet purchased in 1860, box refitted, rams head mark on clasp.

Price: $2,900

Close-up view of the lava cameos and bracelet.

Sharen Duncan-August (D)

Necklace and earrings, circa 1830s, cut steel.
Price: $2,400

Back view shows construction of cut steel.

Section II

1840-1850s Timeline

1840—Queen Victoria weds Prince Albert on Feb.10.

1840—Postal service starts in England.

1840—Electroplating is patented by Elkington of Birmingham, England.

1840s—Machine-stamped repoussé replaces cannetille work.

1840s—Scottish jewelry very much in vogue.

1840s-1850s—Cemeteries begin to be popular in the United States and in England.

1840-1850s—Fabric belts with rectangular vertical buckles become very fashionable.

1840s-1850s—Lockets become popular for the new daguerreotypes. These are deep enough to contain the thick glass used in the photographic process and are usually larger in scale to balance off the full skirts.

1840-1880s—Revolving brooches in vogue.

1841—Gutta-percha comes on the market in November in England.

1841—In America, the Revenue Bill is passed by the Senate. This legislation raises the duty on imported finished pieces of jewelry.

1845—Tiffany's unveils its first catalog.

1845—Irish potato famine begins.

1845—Queen Victoria and Prince Albert buy Osborne House on the Isle of Wight with their private funds.

1846—Prince Albert begins to redesign and rebuild Osborne House.

1848—Victoria and Albert purchase Balmoral Castle in the highlands of Scotland with their private funds.

1849—Gold rush in California. It is reported that the mines yield $10 million worth of gold.

1849—Opals are discovered in New South Wales, Australia.

1850s—American fresh water pearls become highly sought after.

1850s—Cameo brooches become very popular, especially in America.

1850s—Gothic elements become popular. They are used by themselves or mixed with rococo designs.

1850s—Hollow and solid mass-produced machine-made chains come on the market.

1851—Thomas Cook starts his famous "Cook's Tours."

1851—Crystal Palace Exhibition held in Hyde Park, London.

1851—Gold is discovered in Australia.

1853—Crystal Palace Exhibition held in New York.

1853—Prince Albert begins redesigning and rebuilding Balmoral Castle.

1854—9ct, 12ct, and 15ct gold legalized in Britain.

1854-'56—Crimean War between Britain, France, and Russia.

1855—Aluminum, which was at the time considered a very precious metal, is used to make jewelry and also to embellish pieces of gold jewelry.

1857—Indian mutiny against British rule.

1857—Prince Albert made Prince Consort.

1858—Queen Victoria's daughter marries.

1858—Archaeologicial jewelry comes into fashion in America.

1840-1850s

*I*n England the 1840s-1850s were productive and filled with changes. The Postal Service was started in 1840, and that same year electroplating was patented by Elkington of Birmingham, England. In 1854, 9ct, 12ct, and 15ct gold were legalized.

The country was bustling with business except in 1842 and 1848 when there were periods of depression. England was already the undisputed leader in steam navigation and railway construction, and by staging the first International Exposition of Arts and Industry in 1851, she also became known as a patron of the arts.

Those were also very productive years for Queen Victoria. She married her beloved Albert in 1840. In the years from 1840 through 1857 she produced nine children.

The Royal Wedding

Queen Victoria and Prince Albert's wedding took on place on Feb. 10, 1840. The procession set out from Buckingham Palace to St. James and the Chapel Royal where the wedding was to be held. The queen wore a white gown lavishly decorated with custom-made lace and a sapphire and diamond brooch given to her by Albert. He was handsome in his field marshal's uniform decorated with the star and ribbon of the garter, which the queen had presented to him.

The queen left the word "obey" in the ceremony. She rationalized that she was marrying him as a woman, not as the queen. The Duke of Sussex gave her away. The wedding ring was a plain gold one, and at the moment that it was placed on her finger, a cannon fired the royal salute.

After the ceremony they went to the throne room where the marriage was attested to and the couple signed the marriage register. Next the procession went back to

Buckingham Palace for a wedding breakfast complete with a cake that was nine feet in diameter and weighed 300 pounds. [1]

The Queen gave each of the royal bridesmaids a brooch. In his book, *The Beautiful and Illustrious Reign of Queen Victoria*, Rev. John Rusk, Ph.D., describes the brooch in these words: "This brooch was in the shape of a bird, the body being formed entirely of turquoises: the eyes were rubies and the beak a diamond; the claws were of pure gold and rested on pearls of great size and value."

Marriage of Queen Victoria (after the painting by Sir George Hayter R.A.)

The Children

Queen Victoria is said to have worried on her wedding night about having a lot of children, and it turned out that she had a right to be concerned. She proved to be very fertile and quite able to carry children to term.

Nine months after her wedding, on Nov. 21, 1840, she gave birth to a daughter, Victoria, The Princess Royal. Even though it is known that the queen didn't particularly like babies, in less than a year (Nov. 9, 1841), Albert Edward, the heir apparent, was born. Alice Maud Mary was born on April 25, 1843; Alfred Ernest Albert on Aug.

6, 1844; Helena Augusta Victoria made her appearance on May 25, 1846; Louise Carolyn Alberta came along on March 18, 1848; a third son, Arthur, was delivered on May 1, 1850; and a fourth son, Leopold, was born on April 7, 1853. Queen Victoria's last baby, Beatrice Mary Victoria Fedora, was born April 14, 1857.

Victoria may not have liked babies, but she certainly loved having a large family. The royal family sat for many portraits, and their family values were respected by her loyal subjects. When looking at the portraits, remember that the boys and girls were dressed alike in their younger years. The best way to tell which is which is by the hair: The boys' hair was parted on the side and the girls' hair was parted in the center. The exception to this is that the baby, Beatrice, never wore a part in her hair.

Osborne House

After growing up in Kensington Palace, which was rather small, it was not easy getting accustomed to the vastness of Windsor Palace. It contained 700 apartments, but it wasn't suitably arranged to raise the queen's growing family. They were never really comfortable at either palace.

Victoria and Albert decided that it might be nice to have a private residence of their own. Victoria immediately thought of the pleasant times that she had spent on the Isle of Wight. She had visited there twice as a child with her mother. They had stayed at Norris Castle, and she loved the sunshine and being near the water.

Unfortunately that estate was not for sale, but the Osborne House, which was close by, was available. They spent a few days there and decided that it would be the perfect place. Although the old house had 16 bedrooms, they decided to tear it down and build a new one. Albert loved the Italian villa style, and because the area reminded him of Naples, they decided to design the house in that style.

Albert oversaw not only the building of the house but also all of the interior design and decoration. Always aware of the dangers of fire, he insisted that the house be built in wings that could be closed off in case of fire. The basement was built of bricks, and much of the structural

support was constructed with steel. Because the house was being built with personal funds, the couple did everything possible to keep the cost down. The interior walls that look exactly like various types of marble are actually faux painted. The walls are all faux painted plaster and the wooded baseboards are in fact faux painted wood over plaster. This not only was a fire retardant but a cost-saving technique.

The beautiful spiral staircase has cast iron spindles that are painted to look like wood, but the banister is of Cuban mahogany. There was quite a lot of this wood used throughout the house. The ceilings of all the rooms were also lavishly decorated with painted plaster.

Even though they utilized many cost-saving techniques, they made sure that the house was comfortable and suited their needs. Central heating was installed in the basement, and hot water was pushed through pipes with a steam pump. Even with this luxury, it wouldn't have warmed the house by today's standards. But considering that Victoria kept windows open no matter how cold it became, the lack of heat didn't bother her.

In the entry hall there was a speaking tube so that the upstairs servants could be informed when the queen entered the house. The desks, in which she and Albert worked side by side, were equipped with pull cords so they could summon servants without having to get up from their desks. The rooms were all luxuriously furnished with pieces that Albert had chosen. The queen's attitude was that "if Albert liked it, she was happy with it."

Prince Albert had a Swiss chalet built, and that is where the children learned to cook. He also gave each child a plot of ground on which he expected him or her to grow produce. He taught them about money by buying their crops at the market price. He exerted a wonderful influence on the children and his loving wife.

The queen spent time each day riding and enjoying the fresh air. When there was paperwork to do, she enjoyed having a desk and chair set up under the shade of her favorite tree. Here she was attended by at least two of her Indian servants.

On their trips to Osborne House, the royal family always brought at least 100 servants as part of their entourage. Queen Victoria had three full-time lamplighters to light candles and to keep oil lamps filled.

The kitchen was in the basement, as far away from the dining room as possible. Queen Victoria and most of her family never liked to smell food cooking. The food had to travel 100 yards before reaching the serving area where the chef would put on the finishing touches before serving it upstairs. No doubt the food was often cold after making the journey. The queen also had the reputation of being able to eat a five-course meal in 30 minutes. This often caused problems for her guests because when the queen finished eating, all plates and dishes were removed from the table whether or not the guests were finished.

In the beautiful surroundings of Osborne House, the queen and her family spent from two to three months each year. They loved the fact that they had complete privacy and a beach all to themselves.

A partial view of Osborne House on the Isle of Wight.

Balmoral Castle and Scottish Jewelry

In 1842 the queen and her beloved Albert visited friends in the highlands of Scotland. They were enchanted with the area and its people. The queen loved the fact that it was even farther from the constrictive life that she led at Buckingham Palace. She also enjoyed the freedom and fresh air that she experienced. The country and the people reminded Prince Albert of his native Germany. He also enjoyed the many opportunities for hunts that the area offered. After another visit in 1847, they decided it would be the perfect for their second private residence.

In 1848 the queen and Albert visited Balmoral Castle. It didn't take them long to decide that this was the place that they wanted to buy. The price for the castle and 4,500 hectares (a bit over 11,000 acres) was £31,000. The only problem was that the house was entirely too small for the royal family. Prince Albert set about making plans for a new, larger one. In 1853 the queen proudly set the cornerstone for the new castle. The prince had overseen the entire project and, consequently, the queen considered everything to be perfect.

By this time Queen Victoria had her own private royal train. The train took her as far as the tracks went at that time, and horse-drawn carriages were used to continue the journey to Balmoral. The queen did not mind this because it ensured her privacy.

The royal family could lead as close to a normal life as possible at Balmoral Castle. The queen had her prince all to herself, and the responsibilities of Buckingham Palace seemed far away. The queen often referred to Balmoral as her "dear paradise of Royal Deeside."

Here is another view of the house that Albert designed. Pictured in the foreground is Victoria's favorite tree. She is said to have spent a good deal of time sitting under it reading and attending to state affairs. Of course the queen would never just sit on the ground underneath the branches as other people might. Instead, she usually had an open tent erected to protect her from the elements. Her desk and chair were set up there, and she was usually attended by one or two of her Indian servants.

Balmoral Castle

Queen Victoria loved Scotland and all things Scottish. At a state ball in Buckingham Palace, celebrating the opening of the Crystal Palace Exposition, the royal children wore tartans and the guests wore Stuart tartans. It wasn't long before people in England and America were wearing tartan plaids. Some also wore flexible arm bracelets enameled with matching plaid designs. When the queen visited the emperor and empress of France in 1855, her entire family wore tartans. The empress was fascinated with the tartans and she introduced them to Paris.

Queen Victoria's pride in her Stuart ancestry and the popularity of Sir Walter Scott's novels made all things Scottish in vogue. This was especially true of Scottish jewelry. Not only was it the perfect souvenir of Scotland, but by the time of the Exposition of 1862, Scottish pieces were recognized as a fashion statement. They were no longer just considered as mementos of a visit to Scotland.

Brooches and pins were the most popular form of Scottish jewelry. Mountings were usually silver, but some gold and even enamel were used. Moss agate, jasper, bloodstone, cornelian, and other stones native to Scotland were popular. The most popular stone by far was the cairngorm, named for the Cairngorm Mountains of Scotland, in which it is found. This smoky yellow quartz is often incorrectly called smoky topaz or Scotch topaz.

Today Scottish jewelry is very collectible and is commanding high prices.

A Scottish brooch.

The Crystal Palace-London

The Crystal Palace Exhibition in London in 1851 was a showplace for the industry in arts of all nations. In January 1871, this is what *Ballou's Monthly Magazine* had to say about this 1851 exhibition:

In 1851, Joseph Paxton, ornamental gardener to the Duke of Devonshire, who from a very humble beginning had won the favor of the duke and been promoted by him to be principal gardener and architect at Chatsworth, submitted plans for the erection of a palace, of iron and glass, in Hyde Park, for the accommodation of the World's Fair about to be held in London. The plans, the most stupendous of modern time, were accepted, and the palace erected, that fulfilled all the expectations of the architect and the people, and realized for England a measure of fame that her public acts had failed to give her for many years. Paxton was knighted, and the world honored him.

The opening of the Great Exhibition, Hyde Park, London (fashioned after the picture by Eugene Lamé).

The Great Exhibition of the Industry of All Nations' purpose was to provide an arena for the celebration of the arts and industry of man. Each country displayed its newest and best in four divisions: raw materials, machinery and mechanical inventions, manufacturers, sculpture, and plastic art. Prizes were awarded in each category.

Prince Albert was the force behind the creation of this wonderful exhibition. There had been other exhibitions, but this was the first of international scope. *The Crystal Palace Exhibitions Illustrated Catalogue* speaks glowingly of his help:

But indeed, for his (Prince Albert) indefatigable perseverance, his courageous defiance of all risks of failure, his remarkable sagacity in matters of business, and the influence which attached to his support the whole project, notwithstanding the great exertions which had been made to secure its realization, must have fallen to the ground.

This vase was displayed at the Crystal Palace.

The queen and her husband presided at the official opening on May 1, 1851. The Archbishop of Canterbury gave the invocation and a huge, combined choir sang the Hallelujah Chorus. The procession was regal. Clearly, this was the event of the decade, and only season ticket holders were allowed to attend this ceremony. An estimated 25,000 people were present.

After opening day, the general public was welcome. Using England's excellent railroads, they flocked from all over to see the Crystal Palace and its contents. It was the place to see and be seen in. Many days were required to view the exhibition properly, as there were literally miles of things to see. For a small fee, the average workingman or -woman could gaze at sights normally reserved for royalty.

Each country had a section in which to show the best of its machinery, inventions, art, and products. There were musical instruments, furniture, carpets, vases, china, laces, clocks, watches, toys, stained glass, and much more. The jewelry and precious stones attracted much attention. The 280-carat "Koh-i-Noor" diamond and Adrian Hope's 177-carat diamond were on display, along with everyday items such as chatelaines and brooches.

Watches were also very much in evidence. The beautiful timepieces drew attention from all walks of life. Even those who couldn't afford these lovely objects still could appreciate their beauty and admire their works.

Patek & Company's display caught the attention of Queen Victoria. She purchased a small (30 mm in diameter) lady's watch. Even though she had several watches, this one fascinated her because it did not need a key for winding or setting. This was the only keyless watch that she owned. Prince Albert also purchased a Patek watch. Needless to say, these purchases added to the credibility and prestige of this company.[2]

A.W.N. Pugin, the Englishman who designed the new Westminster Palace, designed the medieval court section of the exhibition. Here he displayed the jewelry collection he had designed using Gothic motifs. There were bracelets, brooches, earrings, and necklaces featuring lovely blue and green enameling. They were encrusted with pearls, turquoise, and cabochon garnets (cabochon-cut stones in a medieval-style setting were popular). These ecclesiastical, medieval designs appealed to the romantic nature of the Victorians. The novels of Sir Walter Scott had enticed their imaginations to medieval times. This jewelry made tangible the beauty already associated with that period. The collection caused a revival in enameling techniques. Crosses, quatrefoils, and many other architectural details became popular jewelry motifs.

Jewelry designs based on nature were very much in evidence at the exhibition. Pieces done in natural motifs with flowers set with gemstones and embellished with brilliantly colored enamel leaves were displayed throughout the jewelry exhibitions.

The Crystal Palace Exhibition was a success from every point of view. The queen and royal children enjoyed it so much they visited many times. This was an added incentive for the public. It was estimated that more than six million people visited the exhibition.

For those wondering whatever happened to this beautiful greenhouse-looking building, the *Ballou Magazine* from January 1871 provides this answer:

The Hyde Park structure was so splendid that the people were reluctant to have it destroyed, and it was accordingly taken down and the material transported to Sydenham, in the county of Kent, on the London and Craydon railroad, six miles from London, where it was again put together, and forms one of the most attractive objects of attention to tourists. Morford says "it rivals the British Museum in the wonderful variety of its collections, and yet nothing within the building can compare with the wonderful size and beauty of the creation of glass and iron itself. The grounds are only second to the building in beauty; and scarcely a day occurs, in summer, that some musical festival is not given in the afternoon, enabling the visitor to combine two enjoyments."

Recently it was made the scene of a grand charitable festival—dramatic, musical, and acrobatic—attended by the Prince of Wales and many of the nobility, and the charities were received in little purses, or bags, laid at the feet of the Princess of Wales; and so numerous were they that my Lord Abercorne found as much as he could do, with his cane, to thrust them into position. The occasion was a benefit of the Royal Dramatic College fund, of which the queen is patron, and the attendance was fully twenty thousand. A large part of these, however, were season ticket-holders, but the receipts were very large. Each year some exhibition has been held for the benefit of this organization, until people have grown weary. The present was a happy suggestion and complete success.

The "Palace" belongs to every class, and all can enjoy themselves within its delightful precincts just as the humor suits. Throughout its vast extent the keenest point of individual satisfaction can be realized and at a cost that suits the humblest resources. It is undoubtedly the cheeriest place of popular resort about London, and the managers, from their tact, skill and variety of enterprises, are well entitled to that commendation which an appreciative British public are not chary to bestow. In all seasons the Crystal Palace affords a genial welcome to every description of comer; but it never wore a more smiling aspect than when its portals were thrown open to the sacred cause of charity. At such times all the best influences on human conduct are in their full radiance, and the heart, beating to the noblest of impulses, receives that liberal and well-earned tribute of gratification which endows it with strength to beat on in the performance of equally important duties.

The palace was enjoyed for many years. Unfortunately it was destroyed by fire in 1936.

The only thing that survived in the Sydenham location near Greenwich is the Crystal Palace Dinosaur Park. When it opened in 1854, Queen Victoria and Prince Albert were in attendance and duly impressed with its stone inhabitants. The 28 dinosaurs are scattered over the two islands on the park's lake.

Another Royal Wedding

Queen Victoria's first-born, Victoria, married Crown Prince Fredrick III of Prussia on Jan. 25, 1858. It made news, not only in Europe, but also in the United States. The *Godey's Lady's Book* for 1858 covered the story:

It is to be supposed that most of our city readers are already familiar with the details of this imposing fete, through the columns of the daily papers; but by far the greater part of our subscribers are out of the reach of these ordinary vehicles of information, and for their benefit, as well as a matter of historical curiosity for future reference, we give place to the chief items of feminine interest.

The Wedding Presents

As it is impossible to give the entire list of this all-important display, we select the most costly articles or the admiration, but we trust not envy, of our republican brides that are and are to be.

The most conspicuous among the brilliant mass was the present of the **King and Queen of Prussia.** *A lofty open coronet of diamonds, the design of which, with its spires of brilliants and open shell work between, is probably one of the most chaste and graceful that has ever been executed. Equal with this are those given by Her Majesty. The first is a broad diamond necklace, with treble row of the most brilliant drops and long pointed terminals, which match the light tracery of the coronet. The second gift from the* **Royal Mother** *consists of the three massive brooches, somewhat in the style and size of the Scotch plaid brooch, but which, instead of having an open circlet in the middle, are in each case filled with a noble pearl of the very largest size and purity of color. The* **Prince Consort** *gives a superb bracelet of brilliants and emeralds, which is beautiful, both in design and execution, and is altogether a most costly present. This has additional interest in the eyes of visitors from its being one of the bracelets, which the young bride wore, at the Royal Chapel. That which she wore on the left arm was also a diamond and emerald bracelet, presented by the gentlemen of the Royal Household, but which, though a splendid present, and probably equal in value to the Prince's, is much inferior to it in design, and still more so in the manner in which it is set.*

The gift of the **Prince of Wales** *is in rich beauty of effect far superior to them all. It is a suite of earrings, brooch, and necklace of opals and diamonds; but the opals, in play of color and iridescence, are superior to any we have yet seen, and the design of the settings is quite in keeping with the exquisite beauty of the stones they enclose. As we have said, in magnificent, and at the same time chaste effect, this gift surpasses all. But the* *present of the bride-groom is perhaps the most costly, though in appearance the most simple of any. It is a necklace of pearls, and our readers may easily judge of their value when we say that the necklace, though full sized, only requires thirty-six to complete the entire circle, which graduates in size from the centre, tapering less and less in size of jewels as it approaches each end. The three centre pearls in this superb circlet are said to be of great value.*

The Queen *gives a third present of three silver candelabras, which form the most regal-looking group in silver we have ever seen. The centre piece springs from an elaborate base, and is surrounded by large groups of figures exquisitely chased in full relief. This supports between twenty and thirty branches, and is four feet high. The two others are to match the centre, and are equally elaborate and almost equally massive and lofty. There was no ticket to indicate whom this was given to, one of the authorities stating most positively that it was a present from the queen to the bridegroom; while another asserted that it was presented to the bridegroom's father. As, however, the former statement seemed infinitely more probable, we must believe it to be the correct one. The **Princess of Prussia** gives a truly regal gift of a stomacher brooch of brilliants. The stones in the superb ornament are large and of the purest water; and the setting and design are exquisite. The **Princess Alice** gives a small but beautifully formed brooch of pearls; and the **Princesses Helena, Louisa, Victoria** give each a massive stud brooch or button, similar in shape to those in diamond and pearl of the queen's gifts, which we have already mentioned. These brooches are of massive gold, ornamented with pearls and emeralds, pearls and rubies, and pearls and sapphires. The **Duchess of Cambridge** gives a noble bracelet of diamonds and opal, and the **Princess Mary** her portrait in massive gold frame and stand. One of the most beautiful of all, however, is the gift of **the bride's royal father-in-law, the Prince of Prussia**. It is a magnificent necklace, with pendants of exquisite design. It is composed of pure brilliants and turquoises, and is called, from the size, rarity, and value of the latter gems, the turquoise necklace. **The bride's grandmother**, the venerable **Duchess of Kent**, gives a most magnificent and useful present. It is a large and most costly dressing-case, containing sufficient articles to fit out the toilet-tables of a*

dozen ladies of quality, and all of which are of massive silver gilt enriched with bright red coral. The simplicity and exquisite beauty of the designs for these things are not to be surpassed.

*Next, probably, to this in costliness, though infinitely reduced in regard to size, is the gift of the **Maharajah Duleep Singh,** which is one of the most fairy-like opera-glasses ever used by lady. The design is elaborate—arabesques of gold on white enamel, with a double border and enrichment of diamonds. In a little card-box, with a delicate fringe left out to show the pattern, is the gift of his Majesty the **King of the Belgians**. It is a Brussels lace dress made expressly for the young bride, and our readers will be best able to judge of its exquisite beauty and carefully elaborated workmanship when we state that it is valued at no less than 50,000f., or £2,000 sterling. The **Duchess of Saxe-Weimer** gives a magnificent bracelet of rubies, diamonds, and emeralds, and the **Duke and Duchess of Saxe-Coburg** give plain gold bracelets with enamel miniatures of the givers on each.*

Please note that the bride's dress was trimmed with lace containing medallions of roses, shamrocks, and thistle. The rose would signify England, the shamrock for Ireland, and the thistle for Scotland. Even in her wedding dress, she was being politically correct.

As you can see, most of the gifts were jewelry for the bride. If one is going to live in a castle, one probably doesn't need anything for the household. Also, jewelry has always been considered portable wealth by the royals.

The United States

In the United States, the years 1840-1859 were filled with the excitement of productivity. The fruits of the Industrial Revolution were bringing about new social and economic traditions. In America, Yankee ingenuity was running rampant. Goodyear patented his rubber-making process in 1844, and Howe invented the sewing machine in 1846. In 1849 Tiffany opened his first store, and the gold rush began in California. The American watch industry began to mass-produce watches with interchangeable parts in the 1850s. For those who needed a little leisure time, the National Association for Baseball Players was formed in 1858.

The country was vast, and in that time period, land equated to wealth. When gold was discovered on Jan. 24, 1848, in California, the eyes of the world turned toward Sutter's Mill, and hordes of people headed in that direction. They went by wagon, by horse, and by foot to seek their fortunes. This migration led to new towns all across the country. California's population increased 2,500 percent in one year.[3]

As a result of this migration, coupled with the earlier expansion of the Northwest Territory, railroads were expanding. As the country grew, so did the need for transporting goods and people. In 1840 there were 3,000 miles of track. By 1860 the total had grown to 30,000. Railroads were definitely on the move, bringing economic success along with them.

From Godey's Lady's Book, *summer 1850, "The Train is Coming." If you look on the far right, you can see the train crossing over the bridge. These ladies were not waiting to catch the train; they were waiting to catch sight of the train. Trains were still a novelty, so people went out to experience the sight of the powerful pieces of machinery going by.*

Marriage of the Princess Royal (after the picture by John Phillip, R.A., by permission of L.H. Lefevre, proprietor of the copyright).

The 1850s saw the beginning of the American watch industry. Aaron Dennison had a dream of producing machine-made watches with interchangeable parts. Within a few decades, America became the leader in the mass production of this type of watch.

These years also saw growth in the development of jewelry manufacturing in this country. In 1841 the Senate passed the Revenue Bill. This legislation raised the duty on imported finished pieces of jewelry. The resourceful jewelry industry responded by making and finishing their own jewelry and only importing the parts that were necessary. Boston, Philadelphia, and New York were known for their fine retail jewelry stores. Newark, New Jersey, New York City, and Providence, Rhode Island were important centers of jewelry manufacturing.

The economy had its ups and downs. A business recession in 1856 was responsible for many companies going bankrupt. But hope springs eternal, and this recession didn't keep other people from going into business. Fortunately, this country has always had a good supply of optimism.

New York Crystal Palace Exhibition of 1853

In 1853 the United States had the unoriginal idea of having its own Crystal Palace Exhibition. It was based on the design of the original in London, but on a smaller scale. Set up in Central Park, its promoter was master showman P.T. Barnum.

A delegation was invited from England to participate in the opening ceremonies. Prince Albert was expected to attend, but illness kept him from traveling. Nevertheless, the official representatives from England were presented with a gold dollar coin in a custom-made and engraved ivory box.

(I now own that very box containing the uncirculated coin. It was included in a lot that I purchased at the Duchess of Windsor Auction in Geneva, Switzerland.

At the time I wondered why the duke and duchess had been given the coin that had been originally owned by the duke's grandmother, Queen Victoria. Even more importantly, why had they treasured it until their dying days? Research in old copies of the *New York Times* of 1853 told the story of the coin being given to the delegates to deliver to the prince. Later I realized that the duke may have seen the tiny coin when he was a child. By chance I later found out that the monogram on the tiny ivory box had been used by the duke as his cipher. When he relinquished the crown, the title "Duke of Windsor" was given to him. Since there had never before been a Duke of Windsor, he used the design on the box that had originally been engraved to designate the House of Windsor to be his. This design was used on his note cards, personal items, and even on bed sheets and pillowcases.)

The American version of the Crystal Palace was also a success. It enabled visitors to be exposed to items and people that they had never experienced. Unfortunately, the building suffered the same fate as the one in London: It was destroyed by fire.

Fashions of the Day

Godey's Lady's Book July 1840

Chit Chat of Fashions

At a late drawing room held by **Queen Victoria***, Lady Dinorbin, late Miss Smith (no relation to our Mr. Smith) wore the following splendid dress.*

Costume de Coeur, a splendid white pompadour satin train, sprigged with rich gold and coloured boquets, and trimmed with rich gold dentil; a rich white India muslin dress, embroidered with fine gold, and trimmed with two Volant's of rich gold dentils, over white satin Head dress, plume of feathers, with rich gold dentil lappets and diamonds.

The dress of D'Israelis' wife was also very rich, at the same time remarkable for its simplicity.

A manteau of rich pale green satin, lined with white, and trimmed with blonde; body and sleeves a Medicis, superbly ornamented with a profusion of the finest diamonds; petticoat of tulle, embroidered in a novel and beautiful style, forming bouquets of various colours, a head dress of feathers and blonde lappets; ornaments, a splendid suite of diamonds and emeralds.

The Queen's dress—white net over rich white satin, trimmed with blonde flounces and flowers; the body and sleeves splendidly ornamented with diamonds and blonde; train of silver tissue, richly brocaded in colours (of Spitalfields manufacture), trimmed with silver and blonde, and lined with white satin. Headdress, feathers, diamonds, and lappets.

The Duchess of Northumberland—Manteau of superb lilac satin glacé, lined with silk, and ornamented with a bouffant of satin, with a deep fringe of pearls surrounded with a flouncing of Spanish point lace; corsage of the same, decorated with magnificent point lace, intermixed with pearls; stomacher of diamonds; skirt of lilac aerophane over a rich satin slip of the same colour, glacé, tastefully trimmed with flounces of point lace and fringe of pearls. Head-dress, feathers and point lace lappets, and magnificent tiara of diamonds; necklace and ear-rings en suite.

The Queen could be quite fussy about some things. As you can see from the previous description, it was very much in style to wear feathers in one's hair. It was reported that Queen Victoria insisted that all the women who wore feathers in their hair had to have them upright. Any lady with drooping feathers would not be admitted to her drawing room.

A glimpse at the fashions of the 1840s and 1850s is taken from the viewpoint of the American magazine, *The Designer,* of 1898:

Crystal Palace, New York, 1853

Most important among the vagaries of apparel witnessed by the forties must be reckoned the Bloomer fad, which for a while threatened the whole social system with disruption. An offshoot of the Woman's Rights movement, of which Mrs. Lucretia Mott was the originator and most strenuous supporter, it had its inception in the theory that if women were to be ranked as equal with men, working with them at their several avocations, they must of necessity cast aside the trammels of a costume so manifestly inconvenient and unpractical as that sanctioned by the fashion of the day. In 1849, Mrs. Ann Bloomer valiantly adopted the nondescript costume, which has ever since borne her name, supplementing the innovation by lecturing in New York and elsewhere on its manifold advantages. The costume, which consisted of a jacket with close-fitting sleeves, an abbreviated skirt and a pair of baggy Turkish trousers, was neither graceful nor becoming, and the few doughty feminines who essayed to wear it were pretty harshly treated—not only by the public press, but by the public at large, who mobbed them wherever they chanced to appear. Modifications of the costume were evolved from time to time by progressive women who realized the unhygienic character of the dress of the period, but the remorseless tide of ridicule overwhelmed them all.

One of the curious freaks of fashion contemporaneous with the Bloomer craze was the custom of shaving the hair from the forehead in order to impart imaginary intellectuality to the countenance. Incredible as it now appears, the practice was so widespread among women who aspired to be fashionable that the newspapers and magazines inaugurated a crusade against it; and a brief article published in *Harper's Magazine* of December 1852 refers to it thus:

We have been much grieved of late to observe the growing tendency among ladies to shave their foreheads, in the hope of intellectualizing their countenances, and this occurs more especially among the literary portion of the fair sex. We subjoin a portrait, but mention no names.

The mistake is this. The height of a forehead depends upon the height of the frontal bone—not upon the growth of the hair; and therefore, when the forehead retreats, it is absurd to suppose that height can be given by shaving the head even to the crown. Added to this it is impossible to conceal the blue mark which the shorn stumps of hair still will leave; therefore we hope soon to see the practice abolished.

It was still early in the 1850s when hoops began to reappear, though for several years previously full, wide skirts had been worn over heavy, corded petticoats, which were starched to an alarming degree of stiffness. Popular report ascribes the introduction of the crinoline to the Empress Eugénie, but the actual facts indicate that the renaissance of the hoopskirt began while that beautiful but unfortunate lady was as yet unknown to fame. Nevertheless, in spite of its abuses, the fashion lasted, with variations—of which our final sketch illustrates one that attained high popularity—until about 1866, when its decadence began; but it was not until well into the 1870s that the last remnant of the bustle disappeared, and the furor for skintight garments was initiated.

The Jewelry

Revival! Revival! Revival!

Quite often when things are changing too fast, society looks to the past for inspiration. This was the case with the Victorians. They looked back to the Middle Ages and were enchanted by armor-wearing knights, fair maidens, and chivalry. They wanted to emulate these romantic ideals for their generation. Medieval balls became the highlight of the social circle, giving everyone an opportunity to don the costume of the period. There was even talk of having a medieval ball as part of the queen's coronation, but the idea was dropped because of the enormous expense involved.

As mentioned earlier, this was not the only style from the past to be revived. The Victorians borrowed liberally from many centuries, and there were also revivals of the ancient styles that were stimulated by archeological findings.

Napoleon encouraged the desire to dig after his conquest of Egypt in 1798. From 1806 to 1814 the French excavated the ruins of Pompeii, and their discoveries captured the imagination of the people. The mosaics and the gold jewelry inspired designers throughout the century. In 1848 Sir Austin Henry Layard wrote *Minevia and Its Remains*, a book about the fascinating archaeological finds in the ancient capital of Assyria. These archaeological motifs became popular first in Europe, then in England, and finally in the United States. The United States was always the last to adapt or catch up to the styles in clothing and jewelry. There was always an overlapping of styles. A popular motif in France might take years to develop in America although, as the century progressed and communications improved, this time lapse dissipated.

The archeological revivals continued throughout the century. In the next section we will explore it further.

Garter Jewelry

Before Queen Victoria and Albert took their wedding vows, like most young couples they exchanged wedding gifts. Albert presented Victoria with a beautiful sapphire and diamond brooch, which she wore on her wedding dress, and she gave him a collar of the garter surmounted by two white rosettes and a garter that "was literally covered with diamonds." At the wedding the collar of the garter was worn over his shoulder and the diamond-encrusted garter on his left knee.

King Edward III founded this symbol of chivalry known as the Royal Order of the Garter in 1348 to celebrate his victory over the French and the Scots and to reward his royal supporters. It originally consisted of the king, his son, and 24 knights. Each year they met for three days to celebrate with services, jousting, and lots of eating and drinking.

The king also established the College of St. George to give spiritual support for the college. He gave the college the 13th century chapel, which is the present St. George Chapel at Windsor.

As sovereign, Queen Victoria was the head of the Royal Order of the Garter. Instead of wearing the garter on her knee, she elected to wear it on her arm. Consequently the garter motif began to be used for bracelets, rings, and brooches.

Look for the garter on the queen's upper arm in some of her portraits.

Bracelet with garter motif.

Hairwork Jewelry

Leave it to Victorian women to convert an art created strictly from mementos of the "dear departed" and commemorative pieces to also include love tokens. In those days it was a high privilege to have a part of a loved one near. Since photography was still in its infancy and portraits were very expensive, it's only natural that tangible locks of hair were worn close to the heart. For years this had been a popular sentimental act of love. The treasured lock was usually kept in a special compartment in the back of a brooch, locket, ring, or even in a watch fob.

In the early years of the 19th century, hair became a popular material for the actual making of jewelry. During this time hair was a commody that was more valuable than silver. Because of its value, many pieces of jewelry were made for purely decorative purposes. The following note about jewelry was included in the August 1858 issue of *Godey's*:

> A parure in hair jewelry is also worthy of notice. It is formed of beads or balls of hair, set in bands of black enamel, edged with gold. The parure comprises earring, brooch, an ornament for the frost of the corsage and bracelet.

Hairwork became a drawing room pastime, just as popular as crocheting or tatting in the late 1850s.

What could be more rewarding than working with the hair of a loved one? This type of handwork had spread throughout Europe. In December 1850, *Godey's Lady's Book* introduced it to American women, saying that it had recently "come over" from Germany.

The instructions included how to prepare the hair and how to weave it on a worktable, similar to working bobbin lace. These articles on hairwork jewelry always included patterns for working the hair into various pieces of jewelry.

When the hairwork was completed, it could be sent to the jeweler for fittings. People who supplied fittings and findings for this beautiful work also traveled from town to town. If the local jeweler did not provide this service, the hair could be sent off to New York. Of course, by sending it off, one could never be 100 percent sure that they were getting their loved one's hair returned.

If the lady did not trust her own talents for doing hairwork, there were other methods for obtaining this jewelry. The monthly issues of *Godey's Lady's Book* included illustrations of hair jewelry that could be ordered through the editor. One had only to choose from the many designs and send in the hair along with the proper amount of money.

The other type of hairwork was referred to as palette work: Small pieces of hair made into designs on an artist's palette. The following two photos show examples of both types of hairwork.

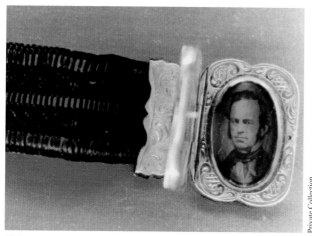

Table-worked hair bracelet with clasp locket containing a daguerreotype. The daguerreotype was developed in 1839, and even though it required the sitter to hold perfectly still for up to half an hour, it was still a popular keepsake. $500

Private Collection

Leila's Hair Museum

Brooch, circa 1840-1860. Gold oval mounting with palette-worked curl and flowers on milk glass background under beveled glass. $350

For those who want to know more about how to make both types of hairwork jewelry and more about its history, check out my book, *The Collector's Encyclopedia of Hairwork Jewelry*.

Bog Oak Jewelry

Many of you are probably wondering just what constitutes the name "bog oak." In spite of its name, bog oak can refer to oak, pine, fir, and yew that has been submerged in the peat bogs of Ireland long enough to be very hard and black.

The first reports of bog oak being used for decorative articles were that of a walking cane decorated with shamrocks given to King George IV in 1821 and a carved tankard presented to William IV in 1830.

Bog oak jewelry is made of this abundant native material and almost always decorated with Irish scenes and symbols. Shamrocks and depictions of the ruins of Muckross Abbey were some of the earliest motifs. In the 1850s the Brain Bour harp was restored and became a popular design. In 1855 carved flowers were introduced, and that same year the Book of Kells-style capital letters started to be used on the jewelry.[4] These motifs were often embellished with other materials from Ireland such as Wicklow gold, Irish silver, Irish rock crystal, amethyst, polished Galway, Connemara marbles, and freshwater pearls from the rivers of Ireland.[5] Irish jewelry was usually worn as a souvenir reminder of a happy visit to a delightful country.

Two pieces of bog oak jewelry, one with a shamrock and the other with a version of Muckross Abbey.

Bog oak brooch with a scene of Muckross Abbey.

Bog oak jewelry was shown at most of the major exhibitions and expositions of the 19th century. Thomas Bennett had a display of it at the 1851 Exhibition in London. Two years later Joseph Johnson displayed pieces embellished with gold, silver, and other stones at the Dublin Exhibition. This was the same man who a year later developed a way to stamp pieces of bog oak using steel dies, pressure, and heat.

Prince Albert's death in 1861 created an instant demand for mourning pieces. Because plain bog oak pieces could be produced cheaply and quickly, the demand for them was strong. By 1865 Joseph Johnson was the leading producer of bog oak items.

Current pieces of bog oak jewelry are much larger in scale and most have a smooth, molded-looking surface. It will never be confused with the old.

Gutta-Percha

In November 1841 a material called gutta-percha was introduced in England. It was a new versatile material that could be molded into items as big as sideboards, statuary, and insulation for underground and underwater cables to items as small as jewelry. *Godey's* stated that when heated, gutta-percha could even be used to fill a decayed tooth.

According to the *Crystal Palace Catalogue* of 1851, "The Isonandra Gutta is the source of the gum elastic known as gutta-percha, one of the most useful substances introduced into the arts during the present century." The sap of a Malayan tree, its usefulness was discovered during the rubber-making process.

At the 1851 Exhibition there were all types of items made of this new natural plastic material, including a sculptural-like group titled "The Deer and Hounds," a huge, highly embellished sideboard, a chaise lounge with a back of gutta-percha elastic, and even printing type.

Because gutta-percha was not only durable but highly impressionable, it lent itself well to the Victorian taste for embellishment. In its finished state, the color is black or brownish black. Its dark color made it a natural material for mourning jewelry, but it was by no means used exclusively for that purpose. Being a lightweight material, it was a popular choice for the large pieces of jewelry that were worn from the 1850s throughout the 1870s.

C. Jeanenne Bell (C)

Gutta-percha bracelet. $350

Vulcanite

Vulcanite is a material that is often confused with gutta-percha. They are both a type of rubber, and the jewelry made from them was often black and used as a less expensive substitute for jet.

Gutta-percha is the sap of a tree that grows in the Malay Archipelago. Vulcanite was made from Indian rubber, which comes from trees that grow around the equator. This sap was mixed with other ingredients, and then mixed with sulphur to harden or vulcanize it. Then it was put into molds and heated to produce a horn-like product known as vulcanite or ebonite.[6]

Vulcanite entered the market as a cheap substitute for jet. It remained popular until the fashion for mourning became passé at the turn of the century.

Most of the jewelry items that we identify today as vulcanite are black pieces made to imitate jet. What most people do not realize is that both vulcanite and gutta-percha were also used to imitate ivory. If white vulcanite and gutta-percha were not confusing enough, the Scottish version of vulcanite was made using guttta-percha as well as Indian rubber.

It was displayed at the 1862 Exhibition in London.

Vulcanite cross. $175.

Vulcanite hand. $95.

Coral

Coral is the calcareous skeletons of marine animals. It is found in abundance near Naples, Italy. The most prized colors are deep red and angel skin pink. Because coral is easy to work, it is used for designs that call for a profusion of flowers and leaves.

The Victorians had a special love for coral jewelry. Since Roman times, coral was believed to possess the power to ward off evil and danger. Consequently, it was a favorite christening present. Any family portrait of the period will illustrate this popularity. Every baby and young child pictured will be wearing a coral necklace. These necklaces were added onto as the child grew. Baby rattles with coral stems and coral teething rings were also popular. As an article in the next section states, the preferred color for coral was deep red.

Coral was not limited to the young. In 1845 the Prince of the Two Sicilies gave his bride, the Duchess d'Aumale, a beautiful parure of coral jewelry. This started a fashion among women of all ages that continued to the late 1880s.

The November 1855 issue of *Godey's* contained this comment on coral: "Coral ornaments are the favorite style of jewelry. The bracelets are formed of strands of coral passing round the arm several times, and finished with a long tassel of the same beads. The bracelet 'sultan' forms a pretty summer ornament; it is composed of strands of gold cord intermixed with green silk and coral beads, wide and worked in a Gothic pattern, from which hang five small coral balls, attached to the bracelet gold ribbons."

Robert Phillips, an English jeweler, did much to popularize coral. He encouraged Italian craftsmen to come to England, and he entered coral jewelry in all of the important exhibitions. This did so much for the economy of Naples, where most coral is found, that the king of Naples honored him for his contribution to the industry.

Many Victorian brooches and earrings were made using natural or branch coral. This was a less expensive way to use the stone. Consequently, there are more of these pieces available than the highly carved ones.

Coral was often imitated by less expensive materials. Elephant and vegetable ivory and gutta-percha were stained and colored to look like coral, which proves that they were quite a bit less expensive. Because elephant ivory was very expensive in the 19th century, coral may have been as costly as diamonds.

Alabaster was also used to imitate coral. The English and French made a coral substitute by treating alabaster with sulfuric acid, grease, and a coloring matter.[7] This imitation coral can be cut with a knife while real coral cannot. This is obviously a destructive identifying technique if not done very carefully in an inconspicuous area. Coral was also imitated in the United States in the late 1870s using a casein-type material.

Please note the amount of coral jewelry shown at the 1862 Exhibition in London. By then the deep red color, which is most popular today, was out of favor and buyers preferred the more pinkish colors.

Coral cameo pendant and a pair of brooches. Cameos of Bacchus, Apollo, and Venus are set in gold and embellished with small diamonds, circa 1854.

Enamel

Enamel is a glass-like mixture of silica, quartz, borax, feldspar, and lead. Metallic oxides are added to produce the desired color. These materials are ground into a fine powder and applied to the article being embellished.

Enamel jewelry was a hit at the 1851 Exhibition. Throughout the 19th century all types of enamel were revived. The art of enameling is a very old technique that requires much talent.

Firing at a temperature of about 1700 degrees Fahrenheit is required to melt the mixture and bond it to the article. Care must be taken because the melting point of the article should be higher than that of the enameling mixture. Each color is fired separately. The color with the highest melting point is fired first. Those requiring progressively less heat are fired in succession. The types of enameling are named according to the method used to prepare the article being decorated. The most popular forms of enameling used during this period were cloisonné, champleve, and basse taille.

For **cloisonné** (kloy-zoe-NAY), or partition, a design is drawn on the article and traced with fine gold wire. This wire forms partitions between which the enamel mixture is poured. Since powdered enamel tends to shrink when fired, several firings are sometimes necessary for each color. After all colors are fired, the enameling is polished until it is flush with the top of the wire.

Brooch, circa 1873, gold with a central plaque with the monogram A&L in cloisonné.

Champleve (shomp-leh-VAY), or "to cut out," is an enamel technique in which the designs are cut out from the background of the metal. The metal between these cut-out areas becomes an intricate part of the design. The hollowed areas are filled with enamel and fired in succession of hardness. After firing is complete, polishing is required to finish the piece.

For **basse taille** (bahs-TAH-ye), or "shallow cut," the designs are cut and engraved in the metal. But instead of just filling these depressions, the entire piece is covered with transparent enamel. Many beautiful designs can be achieved using this method because the color varies with the depth of the design.

Taille d'epergne (TAH-ye de A-purn), an ancient form of enameling, was also revived during these years. For this type of enamel work, a design was deeply engraved or cut into the metal and filled with powered enamel. The piece was then fired and polished. Many jewelers could create this type of enamel, which was used extensively in the late 1860s and all through the 1870s. Although any color could be used in taille d'epergne, the Victorian era favored black or blue.

Two gold brooches embellished with taille d'epergne enamel, circa 1870s. Left: $375; right: $425.

The metals used for enamel were as varied as the methods. Copper and bronze were often used for champleve. Gold and silver provided an excellent base for all the enameling techniques. Although the metal used is a consideration when determining value, the execution of design and the clarity of colors are of the utmost importance. A piece that is beautifully done in copper using several enameling techniques can sometimes be more valuable than one in gold using one color and technique.

Metals

Gold Carat or Karat

Gold has been treasured since ancient times. The Egyptians called it the skin of the gods because it was as bright as the sun.

Gold comes out of the ground yellow and soft. In fact, in its purest form (24k), it is too soft to be suitable for most jewelry. Consequently, other metals such as silver, nickel, zinc, and copper are added to pure gold to make it harder. The percentages of these other metals determine the karat (k) of the gold. Eighteen karat gold is made up of 750 parts of gold and 250 parts of other metals. The color of these added metals determine the color of the gold. For instance, pink gold is made by adding a mixture of silver, zinc, and copper. The depth of the pink color is determined by the amount of copper used. White gold is a mixture of gold, nickel, and zinc.

In Europe during this time period, 18k gold was the standard. In England 9ct and 15ct were legalized in 1854 so jewelry made after this year could be 9, 15, or 18ct. (Please be aware that the English use the abbreviation "ct" to designate the quality of gold while Americans use "k." To make matters even more confusing, the United States uses the word "carat" as a measurement for stones.) American jewelry could be as high as 18k or as low as 8k.

For those whose budget did not include gold jewelry, there were many alternatives. For the look of gold, one could choose gold-plated (after 1840) or gold-filled. Both of these were sold under the heading of "imitation gold."

Before the metals stamping act of 1906, some jewelry manufacturers used trademark-type symbols to designate gold content. These can often be very misleading.

ROGERS, THURMAN & CO. 38 TO 44 MICHIGAN AVE., CHICAGO.   109

FINE SOLID GOLD SHELL RINGS
PLEASE READ CAREFULLY.

Advertisement, circa 1898. Note the mark inside the ring on the upper right-hand side of the page. Anyone receiving this ring as a gift would assume that it was 18k gold. These rings are all gold-filled or, as they called them, gold shell.

Advertisements were worded so that people often believed that they were buying gold. Many rings from the last quarter of the century were marked "solid gold" when they were not. In fact some pieces marked "solid gold" are actually "rolled gold" or gold-filled. Even these terms are somewhat confusing.

Electroplating, Electro-gilding, or Gold-Plating

Electroplating, electro-gilding, or gold-plating sound as if the piece should have a gold plate or sheet of gold covering it. Instead the entire piece is made of a base metal and then a very thin coating of gold is applied. This electroplating process was first used in the 1840s. Consequently, some very old electroplated pieces can be found.

Gold-plated pieces can often be detected by a close examination of the places that get the most wear. Because the coating of gold is thin, the wear points usually show signs of wear that are easy to detect on old pieces.

Gold-Filled or Gold Shell

Gold-filled is a confusing term. Its name implies that the item is filled with gold. Not true! Think of gold-filled as a sandwich made up of a sheet of gold, a sheet of base metal, then another sheet of gold. The piece of jewelry is made from this sandwich. The metal touching your skin is gold, but it has the added strength of the base metal. Sometimes the piece will be made with only a gold top and a sheet of base metal. The thicknesses of the top and bottom sheets of gold determine how long a piece will wear.

Stamped Metal

The stamped metal that was so prevalent in the 1840s was not a new thing. Stamping designs by mechanical hammers began in the late 1760s and was used in jewelry manufacturing since 1777.[8] Stamped metal came into use in the early 1840s because, by stamping out the metal, a detailed dimensional piece of jewelry could be made using a minimum amount of material. During this time period, a stamped piece of jewelry always had an attached back. This construction was referred to as hollow gold even if the pieces were just gold-plated or gold-filled.

After gold was discovered in 1848, it was more plentiful and there was less need for this type of construction for gold pieces.

The Fashions

Here are some fashions taken from women's magazines of the era. *Graham's Magazine, Peterson's Magazine,* and *Godey's Lady's Book* were popular magazines throughout the 19th century. These fashion plates were hand colored and continued to be so throughout the 1880s. Then we will visually explore the jewelry that was used to accessorize these fashions.

Godey's Lady's Book *February 1840 fashions. Note that one lady is doing needlework and the other is ready to open a valentine.*

Godey's Lady's Book *fashions for 1840. The fashion magazines of the day were not prone to showing jewelry. As you study this plate and the following two plates, please note that many of the ladies were wearing brooches. It's almost as if they were saying that it takes a large brooch to complete this new fashion.*

More 1840s fashions from Godey's Lady's Book.

Please note the large brooch in this Godey's Lady's Book *fashion plate.*

Please note the change in the bonnets in this Godey's Lady's Book *1847 issue. The illustration on the right shows the woman wearing a brooch even though the dress already has a bow.*

In Godey's Lady's Book *fashions for December 1847, the ladies are well covered.* Godey's *had the latest Paris fashions, but the magazine Americanized them for the American woman.* Godey's *liked making this point because its competitors,* Graham's Magazine *and* Peterson's Magazine, *specialized in publicizing the latest in Parisian fashions.*

Another Godey's Lady's Book *colored plate for 1847.*

Graham's Magazine, *1847.*

Another Graham's Magazine *plate from 1847.*

An 1848 Graham's Magazine *fashion plate.*

Fashions for January 1852.

Peterson's Magazine *fashions for July 1852. Note the pair of matching bracelets the lady without gloves is wearing.*

Peterson's Magazine *fashions for March 1855.*

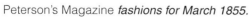

Godey's Lady's *Book fashion plate from February 1859 titled "Here's Another Valentine."*

Godey's Lady's *Book fashion plate from April 1859 "April Fool!"*

Pricing Section
1840s-1850s

Bracelets

Veritas (D)

Bracelet, circa 1852, mourning piece made of table worked hair, engraved on back "Wm Carter died 17th Nov. 1852 age 28."

Price: $450

Photo courtesy Skinner, Boston 9/23/03 (A)

Bracelet, gold, enamel, and diamond book composed of unfolding pages decorated with floral designs in green, blue, and red champlevé enamel, rose-cut diamond binding and crown motifs, 1 g., 7 in., continental hallmark, minor enamel loss.

Price: $1,998

Old World Antiques (D)

Bracelet, circa 1850s, 15k gold love knot motif, hollow gold, 5/8" wide.

Price: $1,300

Code by photograph credit line:

(A) Auction House—Auction Price

(C) Collector—Collector Asking Price

(D) Dealer—Dealer Asking Price

Brooches

Brooch/pendant, circa 1840s, 18k gold mounting centered with a stone scenic cameo surrounded by pearls, 1-1/4" x 1-1/2".

Price: $4,410, £2,450

Messada Antiques (D)

Sharen Duncan-August (D)

Cameo brooch, circa 1840s, silver mounting set with mother of pearl cameo embellished with marcasites.

Price: $400

Brooch, 14k gold mount, set with six faceted oval and elongated pair-shaped foil-backed pink topaz, six faceted oval and cushion-shaped emerald accents.

Price: $1,680

Photo courtesy Skinner 3-16-04 (A)

Charlotte Sayer (D)

Brooch, circa 1840s, painted eye motif on ivory or vellum, 6 cm x 5 cm.

Price: $1,530, £850

Veritas (D)

Brooch, circa 1840s, hollow gold set with amethyst.

Price: $650

Launder Antiques (D)

Back view showing the facets riveted to the back plate.

Brooch, circa 1840s, cut steel, 2" in diameter.

Price: $300, £165

Jeanenne Bell (C)

Brooch, circa 1840, 18k gold snake head and tail with table-worked hair over a hard core, rhodolite garnets embellish the eyes, pear-shaped one is set in a closed back drop, 2" x 2-1/4". Note how the weave resembles snake scales.

Price: $1,200

Brooch, circa 1840s, cut steel, black Vauxhall glass.

Price: $350

Sharen Duncan-August (D)

Messada Antiques (D)

Brooch, 18k gold mounting, set with oval scenic shell cameo, circa 1850s, Roman.

Price: $5,850, £3,250

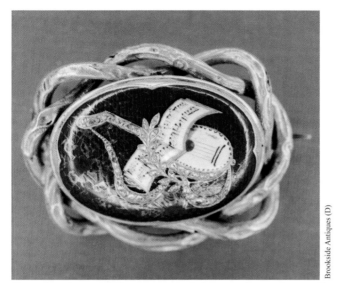

Brooksdie Antiques (D)

Brooch, circa 1850s, enameled lute and music motif embellished with rose-cut diamonds, 1-1/2" x 1-1/4".
Price: $875

Sue Brown (D)

Brooch, circa 1850s, gold mounting set with large shell cameo, fairy carving, rare subject, carved in the Naples area.
Price: $3,600, £2,000

Launder Antiques (D)

Brooch, dated 1860, metal mounting set with scenic shell cameo with charioteer and horses.
Price: $500, £245

Michael Sher (D)

Brooch, circa 1850s, 18k gold mounting, micro mosaic of the Roman Coliseum, black onyx trim.
Price: $2,000

Sharen Duncan-August (D)

Brooch, circa 1850s, high relief cameo carved in coral.
Price: $1,200

Messada Antiques (D)

Brooch/pendant, circa 1850s, gold mounting set with banded agate cameo, surrounded by pearls.

Price: $4,410, £2,450

Photo courtesy Skinner, Boston 1/17/03 (A)

Brooch, circa 1850s, diamond and gem-set, designed as a gloved hand with ruby ring clasping a fan and floral bouquet, bead and prong-set throughout with 213 old mine-cut, pear-shaped, and rose-cut diamonds weighing approximately 9 carats, highlighted by five rubies, 15k gold mount.

Price: $4,406

Launder Antiques (D)

Brooch, circa 1850s, silver gold mount, set with pietre dure.

Price: $540, £320

Michael Sher (D)

Brooch, circa 1840-'50s, gold mounting with piecrust edges, black and white stone cameo, 2-1/2" x 2".

Price: $3,000

Michael Sher (D)

Brooch, circa 1850s, micro mosaic Roman scene, 2-1/2" x 2".

Price: $900

Jewelry Box Antiques (D)

Brooch, circa 1850s, 18k yellow gold shell cameo of praying boy, approximately 3-1/2" x 2".
Price: $1,200

Messada Antiques (D)

Brooch, circa 1850s, 15k gold mounting with micro mosaic Italian scene.
Price: $2,250

Wimpler Antiques (D)

Brooch, circa 1850s, silver mounting with cornucopia motif, set with citrine and different types of jasper, 2" x 1-1/2".
Price: $890, £495

Old World Jewelry (D)

Brooch, circa 1850s, 18k gold butterfly with diamonds, rubies, and emeralds, pin assembly removable, attachment included in case so it can be worn as a hair pin, 2-1/2" x 2 -1/4".
Price: $6,900

Messada Antiques (D)

Pique brooch, circa 1850s, gold and silver inlay, hex-shaped, 2" in diameter.
Price: $945, £525

Earrings

Photo courtesy Skinner, Boston 9/23/03 (A)

Ear pendants, Victorian 14k gold and amethyst, collet-set with one pear-shaped and two oval-faceted amethysts framed by leaves and coiled wire work cones (missing tops).

Price: $1,645

Sharen Duncan-August (D)

Earrings, circa 1860s, cut steel set with painting on porcelain.

Price: $1,200

Lockets

Jeanenne Bell (C)

Locket, circa 1840-'50s, pinchbeck with compartment for photo.

Price: $375

Jewelry Box Antiques (D)

Locket, circa 1840-'50s, engine-turned, gold top case holding two daguerreotypes.

Price: $400

Necklaces

Joanna de Grasse Svensson (C)

Necklace, circa 1840s-'60s, gold snakehead and tail clasp on a table-worked choker.

Price: $700

Photo courtesy Skinner, Boston 9/23/03 (A)

Necklace, Victorian, 18k gold and turquoise, designed as a snake grasping its tail, the engraved head with bands of turquoise highlights, bezel-set ruby eyes, a gold and turquoise drop with compartment verso suspended from the mouth.

Price: $1,410

Photo courtesy Sotheby's of London 12-16-03 (A)

Necklace, gold, turquoise, ruby, and diamond snake necklace, circa 1840, decorated with turquoise scales, the head with cabochon ruby eyes and rose-cut diamond detail, approximately 395 mm long.

Price: $11,880, £6,600

Photo courtesy Sotheby's of London 12-16-03 (A)

Chain, banded agate and enamel, circa 1840, each cartouche-shaped link set at the center with a banded agate within a border of orange, blue, white, and black enamel and connected by enameled floral motifs, approximately 49" long.

Price: $16,200, £9,000

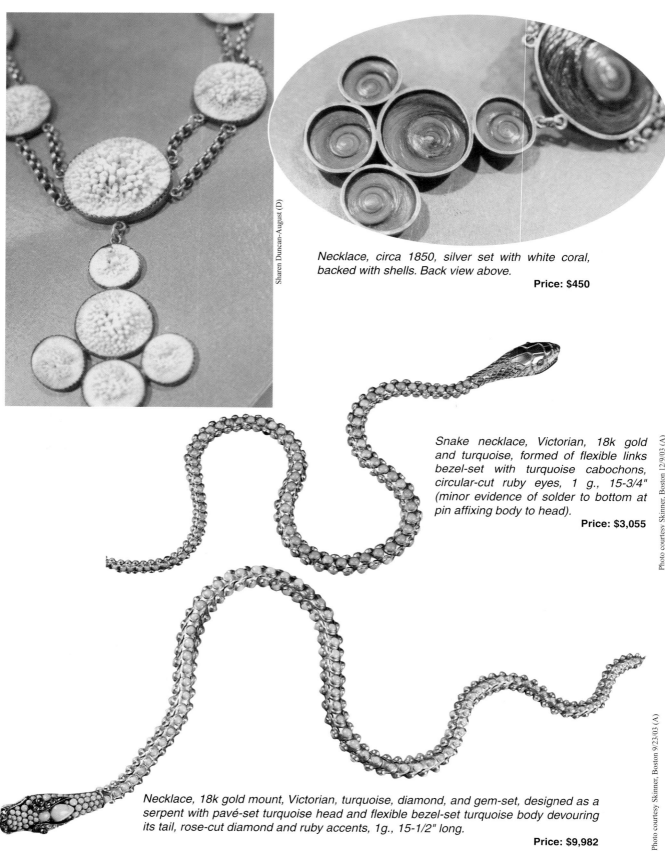

Sharen Duncan-August (D)

Necklace, circa 1850, silver set with white coral, backed with shells. Back view above.

Price: $450

Snake necklace, Victorian, 18k gold and turquoise, formed of flexible links bezel-set with turquoise cabochons, circular-cut ruby eyes, 1 g., 15-3/4" (minor evidence of solder to bottom at pin affixing body to head).

Price: $3,055

Photo courtesy Skinner, Boston 12/9/03 (A)

Necklace, 18k gold mount, Victorian, turquoise, diamond, and gem-set, designed as a serpent with pavé-set turquoise head and flexible bezel-set turquoise body devouring its tail, rose-cut diamond and ruby accents, 1g., 15-1/2" long.

Price: $9,982

Photo courtesy Skinner, Boston 9/23/03 (A)

Rings

Ring, circa 1840s, carnelian cameo, 1-1/8" x 7/8".

Price: $2,850

Ring, circa 1840s, gold mounting centered with circle of rubies and embellished with half pearls.

Price: $756, £420

Ring, circa 1840s, gold mounting set with garnets and emeralds, centered with a pearl.

Price: $792, £440

Ring, circa 1840s, split shoulders, engraved shank, pearls with small emerald, compartment in back for hair.

Price: $774, £430

Side view of ring showing detail on shoulder.

Brookside Antiques (D)

Messada Antiques (D)

Messada Antiques (D)

Messada Antiques (D)

Ring, circa 1850s, 18k yellow gold set with highly detailed stone cameo.
Price: $1,500

Jeanenne Bell (C)

Ring, circa 1850s, gold set with amethyst, rectangular cut with surrounding pearls.
Price: $630, £350

Messada Antiques (D)

Ring, circa 1850s, 18k memorial ring with compartment for hair surrounded by half pearls.
Price: $550

Jane Fletcher (D)

Code by photograph credit line:

(A) Auction House—Auction Price

(C) Collector—Collector Asking Price

(D) Dealer—Dealer Asking Price

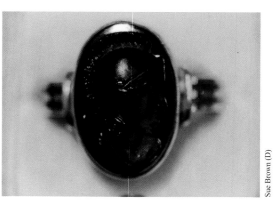

Ring, circa 1850s, carved garnet cameo of Athena, goddess of Athens, locket back, triple gold shank.
Price: $3,290, £1,950

Sue Brown (D)

Sets

Photo courtesy Bonhams and Butterfields 6-24-03 (A)

Code by photograph credit line:

(A) Auction House—Auction Price

(C) Collector—Collector Asking Price

(D) Dealer—Dealer Asking Price

Brooch with a pair of smaller brooches, which were originally earrings, 18k gold Victorian floral motif, the surface embellished with blue and green polychrome enamel, set with round facet-cut garnets, French hallmarks, accompanied by original, fitted box.

Price: $2,644

Pendant and ear pendants, two Victorian 18k gold and amethyst items, pendant designed as a faceted oval amethyst suspending faceted pear-shape amethyst set among high relief scrolling leafy tendrils, together with similar ear pendants (ear pendants with later findings).

Price: $1,763

Photo courtesy Skinner, Boston 9/23/03 (A)

Brooch and earrings, circa 1840s, hollow gold set with garnets and pearls, tops of earrings missing, balls and studs later addition.

Price: $1,975

Jeanenne Bell (C)

Brooch and earrings, circa 1840s, 18k hollow gold set with pearls. **Price: $2,250**

Jeanenne Bell (C)

Brooch and earring set, 14k gold depicting flowering binds, turquoise enamel, garnet and seed pearl accents.

Price: $646

Photo courtesy Skinner 3-16-04 (A)

Section III

1860-1880s Timeline

1860s-'70s —Taille d'epergne enamel embellishment is much in fashion. Favorite colors are black or royal blue.

1860s—Painting on porcelain artists often use black backgrounds for their portraits.

1860s—The Comstock Lode is discovered in Virginia City, Nevada. It is said to yield over $350 million worth of gold and silver.

1861-'65—The Civil War rages in America.

1861—Prince Albert, Consort of Queen Victoria, dies of typhoid on Dec. 14.

1862—International Exhibition is held in London.

1863—Prince Edward marries Princess Alexandria, the daughter of the king of Denmark.

1865—U.S. President Abraham Lincoln is assassinated.

1867—New houses of Parliament are opened.

1869—Diamonds are discovered in South Africa.

1869—The Suez Canal, which has been under construction since 1859, is finally completed.

1869—"The Treasure of Priam," an archeological find, is discovered by Heinrich Schlieman.

1869—The first brokerage firm owned by a woman is opened on Wall Street.

1870s—Matching pairs of bracelets (one for each arm) come back into vogue.

1871—Trade unions are legalized.

1872—British Museum purchases fine examples of ancient jewelry from the Castellani Collection.

1875—Horizontal bar pins become popular.

1876—America celebrates her centennial with a wonderful exhibition in Philadelphia.

1876—Queen Victoria is declared empress of India.

1877—The British acquire controlling interest in the Suez Canal.

1886—Gold is discovered in South Africa.

1887—Queen Victoria celebrates her Golden Jubilee (50 years on the throne).

1889—Congress declares war on Spain.

1860-1880s

The decade of the 1860s began with all the high hopes for the future that most people have for a new year and new decade. In England this optimism was short-lived as far as the queen was concerned. In March 1861 her mother, the Duchess of Kent, died. Victoria was devastated. She had been under her mother's thumb for so many years that the over- protectiveness caused some resentment. When Victoria became queen, the pendulum swung in the opposite direction, and Victoria sometimes demonstrated power over her mother. After her mother's death, Victoria was overcome with sorrow, sadness, and guilt.

She was still in mourning for her mother when death struck again on Dec. 14. This time it was her beloved Albert. He had been on a visit to see about their son, Edward, who, as usual, was not living up to his parents' standards. Albert had become ill, and most reports state that he died of typhoid, but the guide at Osborne House said that they now believe he also had cancer. He hadn't been feeling well for a while and had made a special trip back to Germany to see his family. This and other things that he did the last years of his life lead some to believe that he knew his time was drawing near even though he was still a relatively young man.

Victoria was grief-stricken. The nation was stunned, and almost everyone went into mourning. Victoria's mourning lasted for years. She did not attend his funeral; instead, she retreated to Osborne House where she is said to have slept in one of his nightshirts in the bed that she and Albert had shared. From that day until the day that she died at Osborne House, Albert's side of the bed was turned down each evening, and each morning his basin would be filled with hot water and his shaving set put in place.

Victoria was obsessed to do things as Albert would have wanted them done. The remaining years of her life were dedicated to his memory. She wanted the country to know and love him as she did. Writers were commissioned to record the story of his life. Monuments were built and dedicated to his memory.

A statue of Queen Victoria and her prince.

In the United States the second year of the new decade wasn't any better than that of Queen Victoria's. The first shots of the Civil War were fired in April 1861. Neither side expected it to last long. The mood was almost jovial as the men rushed off to battle, but this changed as the days and weeks turned into years.

With the menfolk away at war, it was even more important for those who remained at home to have a personal reminder of their loved ones. Lockets became an important fashion accessory. Not only could a locket hold a tintype or lock of hair, but it gave an old dress an updated look.

This woman is probably wearing her mother's or grandmother's locket. From its scale it is circa 1860-1870s and possibly silver. It is suspended from its original "book chain necklace." This book chain style was popular throughout the remainder of the 1800s. It is my belief that it was referred to as a book chain because it had a flat back and could be taken off at night and placed as a bookmark in a Bible or other reading materials.

With the development of photography, pictures became more and more popular. Consequently lockets remained in fashion. The locket in this photo is a smaller scale, circa 1870-1880s. It is also on a book chain necklace.

Two women wearing lockets. Book chain necklaces always opened and closed in the front because jewelers in those days understood how difficult it is to clasp necklaces behind the neck. The woman on the left is also wearing a brooch with a key and lock motif. This motif was popular in both gold and silver for bracelets, stickpins, and necklaces until after the turn of the century.

A tintype of another woman wearing a locket suspended from a belcher-style chain.

Lockets were not always round or oval. This square one is also suspended from a book chain.

This book chain locket motif is very typical of the 1870s. Lockets were embellished with black taille d'epergne enamel, and a glazed compartment for hair or a photograph was located in the back.

The war changed the role of women more than anyone could imagine at the time. Many women in the North and the South had to take over the responsibilities that men had previously handled. That included everything from working in the fields to working in an office. With women also involved in the war efforts, rolling bandages or preparing for sanitary fairs, the hair net became an easy way to deal with their hair.

The war also created significant changes in industry. The American Watch Company, which produced a line of lower-priced watches, thrived. In 1861-'62 the company came out with the William Ellery watch, which was a big seller during the Civil War. Any soldier who could afford a watch wanted one to take into battle, where 15 minutes sometimes seemed like hours. The officers also needed to know the time in order to accurately synchronize their attacks. The war also made some industrialists very rich. The watch, a traditional symbol of wealth, was a necessity for this new class of wealthy people.

There was much bloodshed on both sides of the war between 1861 and 1865. The country experienced pain and suffering. It was said that the women would go onto the field after a battle to see if any of their loved ones were dead. The custom was to cover a dead soldier's face with his hat. The ladies would slowly lift the hats and their faces would fill with sorrow even if they didn't know the victim.

Many people came to the realization that a country at war with itself could never have a true victory. Both sides were relieved when the fighting finally came to an end in 1865.

Another crushing blow for Americans was the assassination of President Lincoln. Thousands lined the railroad tracks to pay tribute to the slain president as his body passed by in its railroad car on the way to its final resting place.

Fashions for Mourning

Because life was so fragile prior to the discovery of antibiotics and other medical advances, death seemed close at hand and it usually was. A woman could give birth to as many as twelve children and have only five of them live to age five. This, coupled with a shorter life expectancy, meant that some people were in continuous mourning for years.

Death was a very real and present part of life in Victorian times. It demanded respect not only for the departed, but also for the living. A death was always followed by a period of mourning. This usually consisted of a year spent in full mourning and another in half mourning. Some widows were known to mourn the rest of their lives. During this mourning time, the deceased's relatives were subject to very rigid dress codes. These applied not only to widows, but also to daughters, aunts, sisters-in-law, and cousins.

Godey's Lady's Book helped keep women up-to-date on what was appropriate. Its March 1855 fashion section carried these recommendations:

Mourning attire for a daughter—mourning dress of parametta cloth trimmed with robins of crepe; small crepe collar with cuffs. Walking-Dress—dress of black silk and an overskirt of crepe; crepe collar and sleeves, crepe and silk bonnet with fall, entirely black inside; black parasol; jet brooch and chain; black kid gloves. Attire for an Aunt—black poplin dress for the street; black velvet bonnet and black cloth mantle; white collar and sleeves. Evening Dress— barege or glacé silk flounces; collar and sleeves, with little but rich embroidery; white kid gloves.

Seven years later, in 1862, the styles for full or deep mourning had not changed, but lighter mourning did have a few additions:

Mourning being also subject to the caprices of fashion we will give a few hints as to the styles now in vogue.

For deep mourning, there is nothing new. Bombazines, and all lusterless materials with English and French, grenadines, crepe maretz, and bareges trimmed with crepe, are used for dresses. English grenadine makes a very pretty crepe-like trimming, and it is not so expensive. Shawls like the dresses are much worn. Mantles are of the scarf shape, quite deep at the back, with long square ends in front. They are made of crepe, grenadine, or grenadine barege. Deep mourning bonnets are either of Neapolitan or crepe, with an English crepe veil thrown over them, plaited at the sides of the bonnet, and kept in place by long jet clasp pins.

For lighter mourning, custom permits the introduction of a few colors, such as pearl, gray, lilac, and purple. For light mourning dresses, there are organdies, grisailles, lutongs, satin de Mai, grenadine barege, Chambery gauze, checked silks, etc. The trimmings are various, consisting of flounces, gauffered ribbons, and ruches edged with lace.

1862 Exhibition— London

Even with the sad beginning to the decade, many joyful things continued to occur. One of the pleasant events was the 1862 Exhibition in London. *Godey's Lady's Book*, which was published in Philadelphia, had grown to the point that it could have its own representative at the event. Even though the news was late getting back to the United States, the subscribers were happy and anxious to read about the Exhibition, especially the jewelry courts. Taking the time to read about the jewelry on display at this important exhibition gives one an excellent idea of what was in style or what would be the fashion in the near future. These lines are from the March 1863 magazine:

In glancing at the contributions, honorable precedence is due to those Messrs. Hunt and Roskell. The most remarkable gems in this collection are the Nassuck and Arcot diamonds, belonging to the Marquis of Westminster; a splendid suite of diamonds and sapphires exhibited by permission of the Earl Dudley; a remarkably fine ruby, a Pierre chantillant, set in a tiara, the property of Mr. Holford; and a row of pearl beads, each worth £250. But even more attractive, in our eyes as ornaments, are a parure of diamonds intermingled with very large turquoises of perfect color; another, very delicate, of brilliants and pale coral-tinted pearls; a bouquet of diamonds, consisting of full-blown rose, carnations, fuchsias, and other flowers tied with a ribbon, and mounted springs to form a stomacher; various tiaras of excellent arabesque, star, and scroll patterns; and a dazzling bracelet, with emerald set diamond wise in the centre. Among the smaller objects, which could only appear trifling in such a neighborhood, a brooch and earrings of small diamonds, each representing a leaf with pink coral berry adhering to it, and a moss rose-bud with leaves, also imitated in diamonds, the flower alone being shaped from pink topaz, are beautiful, and should not be passed unnoticed have contributed to the exhibition, besides this fine display of mounted gems, a mill for cutting diamonds, where the process is explained by the superintendent of this branch of their business. It is, of course, well known that the diamond can only be cut by itself. The first step, then, with stones of ordinary size—for very large ones process—is to set them in cement on the ends of two pieces of wood, and to grind them together by hand until something like the desired form is attained; the diamond is afterwards embedded in soft metal, well secured by clamps, and subjected to the action of machinery brought to bear in this wise: A horizontal plate of soft iron, about twelve inches in diameter, well charged with diamond powder and oil, is set in rapid motion, performing upwards of 2000 revolutions per minute; the stone, placed in contact with it at the proper angles, presents in due time the required number of facets, sixty-two in the case of a double-cut gem. This part of the work completed, the same process is continued with diminished use of diamond-powder until the surface is sufficiently polished. Nothing can be more interesting than the illustration which different departments mutually afford, and we have drawn attention to this instance, believing that the exhibition of machinery would become a source of greater pleasure to lady visitors if they viewed it—not per se as a whole, but sought out in it from time to time a practical knowledge of the processes which lead to the results that specially interest themselves.

The privilege of exhibiting the Koh-i-Noor, and the celebrated Lahore rubies, the property of her Majesty, renders the case of Messrs. Gerrard and Co. supremely attractive to the multitude: it is, of course, unrivaled in its display of precious stones. The three large uncut rubies, bearing Persian inscriptions, and set, in India fashion, with fine brilliant drops to form a necklace, now constitute the great subject of wonder, the Mountain of Light being familiar to the public eye, and somewhat reduced from its wondrous size by the further operation of cutting which it has lately undergone, and to which these marvelous rubies must also be subjected before they produce their just effect. In juxtaposition with these are many fine examples of our own more advantageous mod of displaying jewels: parures of diamonds mounted with emeralds, with sapphires, with pearls of divers colors; diamonds arranged in scroll pattern for tiaras; in festoons for necklaces;

diamonds, in short, under every conjunction of circumstances, even representing a lion's head with water, expressed by flexible brilliant pendants, flowing from the mouth, to be worn in the form of a brooch.

The collection of first-class gems exhibited by Mr. Hancock, though rather less extensive than the two already mentioned, can scarcely be classed below them. Here, also, we find stones almost worth a king's ransom, and the style of mounting is in each case so very well designed as to give a remarkably striking character to the ornaments. The most prominent decoration of the case is a complete suite of magnificent emeralds and diamonds. The diadem consists of a very open scroll framework in diamonds, within the interstices of which are nine solid pendent emeralds, increasing in size to the centre, and in their tremulous motion flashing out each moment fresh effects of color. The necklace to match has also nine emerald ornaments, with light settings of diamonds and pear-shaped emerald drops. The brooch is of immense size, and is rivaled only by another, equally large, in which the centre stone is a sapphire of exquisite hue, a second having been found worthy to be a pendant to the first. These are surrounded by a broad arabesque open border of diamonds of simple but most effective design, which forms a complete frame angular on the four sides. Mere verbal description fails to do justice to its beauty, as our readers will admit if they see for themselves. Near at hand are other valuable necklaces, emeralds again, but this time arranged with studied negligence in block fashion; and fine opals with diamond entourage, and five large opal drops. Scarcely less precious than these dazzling jewels are a necklace, stomacher or comb, and head ornament of transparent stone intaglios with classical setting: they are masterpieces of the modern antique. Among the more unpretending ornaments, a brooch of the Louis XIV style, with large pearl and pink coral coupled together with drops, is worthy of admiration, as are likewise of negligee brooch and earrings of diamond form, the centre a chessboard pattern in turquoise and diamonds, with border of pearls, a diamond forming each angle.

The ebony and bronze trophy of Mr. Emanuel, forming so very conspicuous and elegant an object in the nave, is scarcely less thronged with visitors than the three great collections necessarily thrown somewhat in the shade by the excess of light elsewhere. The cheval de bataille in this instance is the emerald brooch mounted in diamonds, valued at £10,000. Passing over a fine suite of opals and diamonds, for such things become almost common in our eyes when we have spent half an hour in the jewelry department, we may particularly refer to an effective diamond and pearl bracelet, with butterfly clasp—the centre, pearl, with diamond and emerald wings—and to the examples here put forth of Mr. Emanuel's spécialité ornaments, made in a kind of pink ivory and gold, inlaid with different gems. This pink substance, closely resembling pale coral, is cut from a rare shell found in the West Indies, and is, from its hardness, susceptible of a high degree of polish, and of being very variously applied.

By no means less noteworthy, though, from its position, less likely to obtain due recognition, is the case of Messrs. London and Ryder, to be sought for in the intricacies of the South Court. Here we find an opal which claims to be the finest in the building. It is not, we believe, the only one with such pretension; but a more perfect specimen of the magic stone could scarcely be desired than the one in question, set as a brooch, with floral margin of brilliants, large emerald drop, and ruby button. Near it, a fine contrast in color, is a wonderful carbuncle, forming a bracelet clasp, which we are well disposed to accept on its own showing as the finest in the world; and a singular heart-shaped pearl which once enriched a crucifix, very large, but more curious than beautiful. The style of a diamond tiara exhibited here, and copied from the antique, is excellent; and another of pearls, lightly set in the form of scallop-shells, with branches of pink coral between, is, to our own thinking, a really covetable adornment. There is also an exquisite bijou in the shape of a carbuncle watch with radii of small brilliants, suspended from chain and brooch en suite. Very delicate to our modern ideas, though barbaric to those of the Greeks, as developed in the collection of M. Castellani, is a bracelet of the lightest pink coral cut into small lily-shaped cup-flowers, with gold stamen tipped with minute gems. This design is also to be met with elsewhere, as likewise the bracelet with revolving clasp pierced to display four small miniatures or photographs, which is somewhat of a novelty. To complete the attraction of this case, we have the Emperor of China's scepter taken at the sack of the Summer Palace, and an illustration of the art of diamond-setting afforded in the progress of a bracelet. First is given the rough design on a card (commonly called the working model); next, the tracing of the pattern in red lines on black wax, with the stones arranged on a section of it; the silver form prepared, mounted and pierced to receive the brilliants; and, finally, the half bracelet completed.

It is not a little pleasant, when due tribute has been paid to the gems par excellence, and our every faculty seems dulled by their dazzling brightness, to pause before the collections of one or two exhibitors, who may be said to have quitted the beaten track in this art and to have sought in its byways a field for their skill. If, for example, the visitor seeks out the standing of Mr. Phillips, its chastened coloring affords relief to the eye, whilst the character of its contents well repays curious inspection. A large division of this case is appropriated to the exhibition of Neapolitan coral, at present held in peculiar estimation as one of the most recherché styles of feminine ornament. Fashion has for once set her approving seal on what is intrinsically beautiful, and ladies whose possessions are limited only by their desires will have reason to congratulate themselves on the power of substituting at will this simple yet finished style of ornament for others which bear more ostentatiously the impress of their value. Pink coral we have there before us in all its manifold varieties, from the delicate hue of the blush-rose to a deep tint of cerise, just falling short of the old-fashioned red of nursery associations, which is scarcely admitted to be kindred with these refined treasures of the deep. The value of each rough specimen as won from its rocky bed is dependent on size, from freedom from flaws, unity of coloring, but above all, on the comparative paleness of its tints; thus a parure consisting of tiara, bracelets, negligee, brooch, etc., of the most tender approach to pink must be regarded as the pride of the collection, though it would be less effective for wear than others of warmer shade which surround it. The beauty of the carving, designed and executed by Italian skill, cannot be too highly praised. The brooches, bracelet, clasps, and other articles of that kind are generally fashioned into beautiful bouquets with fruit forms sometimes mingled by the fanciful taste of the artist, who not seldom finds his inspiration in the material, and, by yielding to Nature's suggestions, produces something worthy to become a model, if not exactly recognizable as an imitation. There are, of course, some examples of coral cameos; the favorite design of cherub's head with wings, and a more appropriate one of sea nymphs at play, are well executed; but this style of workmanship appears to be less in request than the groups of flowers. In the tiaras for the head, composed of branch coral variously arranged, the chief novelty we observed was the introduction of little berries or beads among the branches; and in one instance a combination of white and red, which had a striking appearance. For the information of persons who, like ourselves, have had very inadequate notions of the value of such manufactured coral, we may mention that the price of the coronets ranges from £6 to £30; and that the other articles constituting a complete suite would, if fine specimens, cost about £100. Turning from this division of Mr. Phillips' case, we find in another some remarkable ornaments in antique styles, executed under his own superintendence. Unrivaled in its way is a cinquecento bracelet, opal centre, with elaborate mounting of grotesque masks and many-tinted gems. It is en suite with a small tripod jewel-stand, originally designed for a snuffbox, but finally deemed worthy of more honorable office. In necklaces there are specimens of each one of the classical styles—Etruscan with scarabe; Greek with medallion female heads in English porcelain enamel; Egyptian, copied from the original found on a mummy, by permission of Lord Henry Scott; and also a noticeable collection of Oriental onyxes with cinquecento setting. Nor must we overlook a bracelet formed of a massive gold band into which are introduced the beautiful green Brazilian beetles, which, by a peculiar process of drying, become hard and durable as stone. A variety of brooches, etc., with Roman, Greek, and Etruscan settings, complete this display of modern antiques. There may be diversity of opinion as to the real value of such revivals applied to personal ornament; but the highest fashion of the day sanctions them, and, as works of art demanding research and careful study of detail in their workmanship, they are well worthy of examination.

This is a bracelet from the famous Mr. Phillips of Cockspur Street about which the article speaks so glowingly. His displays must have been most impressive.

The old-established firm of Lambert and Co., well known as producers of fine church plate, has likewise been fortunate in opening out a new style of jewelry peculiar to themselves. They exhibit, besides mounted specimens, a case of crystals, within which the semblance of some brilliant bird or characteristic head of dog, horse, or stag is rendered with the colors and roundness of nature. This effect is gained intaglio of the form and depth required, which is afterwards carefully colored. Only one artist, we believe, can as yet compass this difficult task to perfection. His designs are evidently studies after nature, so that persons who can afford expensive fancies might probably wear in this form the portrait of some individual favorite. This invention is adapted to pins, rings, and brooches. The price of an average-sized crystal intaglio, mounted, would vary from seven to ten pounds.

The crystals that Lambert and Co. displayed were reverse carved and painted by Charles Cook, whose work made him famous.

Messers. Howell and James make a fair show in this as in their departments. They exhibit a small suite of white Sidmouth pebbles with antique setting brightened with small beads of the Marquis of Breadalbane; and a variety of jewelry in the ordinary styles without character enough to claim description. The novelties in Mr. Attenborough's collection are gold ornaments of a large buttercup pattern, the open petals forming a shallow basin with central tuft in jewels; but its best features are a diamond butterfly brooch and an emerald and diamond locket, with green enamel and diamond chain. Messrs.

Widdowson and Veale present large coral cameos mounted in diamonds, amethysts, with brilliants inserted, etc.; a tasteful collection of average value, adapted to the requirements of ordinary purchasers. Colored enamel, beautiful but fragile, is very successfully applied as a background for jewels by these exhibitors; and we must direct attention to a geometrical-shaped reversible brooch, the central part of which turns on a swivel, and the mourning onyx and diamond give place in a second to some gayer device. This idea, susceptible of so many different modes of execution, will be rather attractive to ladies who are indifferent to variety for its own sake, and only desire in their ornaments the change of color which will adapt then to different dresses.

Among the various representations of Scotch jewelry, those contributed by Messrs. Muirhead display native minerals in very attractive dress. A cairngorm brooch, in which the stone is supported by diminutive stags' heads and antlers in silver, is very well designed; and a suite of the same stone mounted in gold inlaid with pebbles, imitative of the popular cinquecento. Such memorials of tours in the north may now, if well chosen, have a value apart from that of association, which was formerly the only one we could attach to them.

Here is a beautiful example of Scottish jewelry set in gold and embellished with native stones. The article states that these pieces were now worn as beautiful accessories and not just as souvenirs.

Railroad Expansion

Railroads played an important role in the Civil War. Ammunition and supplies had to be moved from one area to another, and transportation was needed. The Civil War was the first war to rely on railroads. After the war, homecoming soldiers were acutely aware of the changes. Railroads and industries such as iron and steel were booming. The reconstruction of the South depended on railroads to bring in goods. Business was brisk.

At the same time the railroads desperately needed the returning soldiers in order to expand tracks to the West and populate the land. The Pacific Railroad developed a post-war employment project for returning veterans. It was most successful. An 1865 advertisement for the Illinois Central Railroad Company offered "1,200,000 acres of rich farming lands for sale." They were willing to sell "tracts of 40 acres and upward on long credit and at low prices." Many veterans decided to use their "bonus" money for land and equipment.

In 1869 a golden spike was driven at Promontory Point, Utah, to commemorate the fact that railroad tracks now spanned the continent. What a great accomplishment!

England was also crisscrossed with rails. Because it is only the size of the state of Alabama, it didn't take nearly as long to accomplish this as it did in the United States. But it meant as much to that country as it did to ours insofar as the growth of industry was concerned.

One of the most lasting effects of the railroad in both countries is that it helped change them from being predominately agricultural to industrial. Young rural people saw the city as a glamorous place in comparison to the sparsely inhabited areas in which they lived. Many took the first opportunity that presented itself to leave the drudgery of the farm and become a part of the excitement of the city. This change in demographics was to play an important role in the future of both countries.

The Queen Travels

Sometimes we tend to think of Queen Victoria sitting busily at her writing desk, tending to affairs of the state. In reality, she made many trips prior to the death of Prince Albert. Some visits were considered state visits, and some were motivated by curiosity and other factors.

Whatever the reason, the trips involved an enormous amount of preparation. This preparation was accomplished not only by her staff but also by individuals at the locations to which she was traveling. One such journey occurred when the queen visited Muckross House in Cillarroy, Ireland, in 1861.

Victoria had visited Ireland in 1849 and 1853, but had never been to Kerry. A short synopsis of this trip will give you an idea of the preparations that were made for the queen's brief visit.

The visit was instigated when a family by the name of Herbert invited the queen to its home. Mr. Herbert was a member of Parliament, and he hoped that the visit would eventually bring him and his wife the titles of "lord" and "lady." Queen Victoria had heard about the beautiful home designed by William Burns, a Scottish architect, and built in 1843. She was curious about it and decided to combine a visit to the house with her next state visit to Ireland.

Queen Victoria's acceptance of the invitation was confirmed in 1855 for a visit in August 1861. The Herberts were excited to hear that the queen was coming, and for the next eight years prepared for the visit. The house had been built in 1843, but after twelve years the owners decided it needed a facelift in order to be fit for a queen. They ordered everything from tapestries to teaspoons. The list of custom-made items included a carved sideboard and woven draperies from Paris, and a complete set of musical instruments. New wallpaper was ordered for the billiards room, which was to serve as the private dining room for the royal family. They also had a desk custom-made for Queen Victoria. Outside improvements included a new driveway and shrubs and flowers.

The Herberts prepared to give up their downstairs living quarters to the royals. They were notified that Queen Victoria needed a downstairs room with a window and a fire escape. Consequently, a fire escape was built. It's not clear whether Queen Victoria was afraid of fire or if Albert had insisted on the fire escape. He tended to be very protective of his wife.

The Herberts had also been told that the queen would be bringing her own bed and 100 servants. It's been said that many in the queen's entourage had to stay in nearby homes. This helped establish Irish bed and breakfast houses.

Queen Victoria and her party arrived in Killarney at 6:30 p.m. on Monday, Aug. 26. They spent the first night with Lord Castlerosse at Killarney House and the next day traveled to Muckross. They reached the house around 6:30. The following is an excerpt from a letter written by Eleanor (one of Herbert's daughters) to her Aunt Jane:

> It was a glorious evening and the finest sunset I ever saw…the steps were covered with red cloth and Mama went to the carriage door with Papa to receive the Queen…after standing a few minutes admiring the view from the Library window the Queen expressed a wish to go to her rooms which were Mama's. [1]

The Royal Party spent two nights at the home and left at noon on Aug. 29. Unfortunately, the Herberts never received their titles. The untimely death of Prince Albert in November of that year and Henry Herbert's health problems made it impossible.

1876—The Centennial Exposition

In 1876, America celebrated her 100th birthday with a huge exposition in Philadelphia. It drew exhibitors from all over the world and offered Americans who had

had very little, if any, opportunity to travel outside of the country a chance to see new and exciting things from strange and wonderful countries.

Each country tended to display the very best of its products. It was the perfect setting to show off what Yankee ingenuity could accomplish. New products, such as Alexander Graham Bell's telephone, the new electric light, and the typewriter were briefly noted because most visitors could not see a real need for these things. The attention-grabbers were the huge machines that were displayed and demonstrated. President Ulysses Grant and Emperor Dom Pedro were there to start the huge Corliss steam engine. It is noted that when they opened the throttle "they felt that they had indeed witnessed the wonder of the age."

This attention to machines was exactly what the American watch factories were hoping for when they not only brought examples of their finest machine-made watches, but also pieces of machinery to demonstrate the parts being made. Any watch factory that could possibly afford it wanted to show at this exhibition. It would not only add prestige to their product, but it would be a perfect opportunity to acquaint people with their name and product. For the first time the visitors would see beautiful machine-made parts that were as good as or better than handmade ones. Seeing is believing, and many realized that machine-made products were no longer to be considered inferior.

There were many jewelry displays at the Centennial, but none as striking as the Tiffany exhibit. That display was filled with watches, silver, jewelry, and stationery. Tiffany not only received special recognition but also was presented with a gold medal.

The Centennial celebration had many positive results. The nation took pride in its achievements and was favorably recognized by the rest of the world for its famous Yankee ingenuity. Even more important was the contact with other countries' cultures that the exposition allowed the average person.

Reverse painting from the glass of a clock made as a souvenir of the Centennial Exposition. It depicts one of the buildings housing the exhibition.

Fashions in Clothing

Godey's Lady's Book, 1862

Chitchat upon New York and Philadelphia fashions for August.

Our chat this month begins with an echo of the chat of all the fashionable ladies of Paris-Le Jupon Impratrice. The marvelous petticoat invented by the fair Eugenie herself. It is described as being made of cambric muslin, starched as stiffly as possible. Its circumference is six yards at the widest point, and it is covered by nine flounces of still greater circumference. The lowest of these flounces is a mere frill; the second, a few inches longer and wider, completely covers the first; the third does the same to the second, and so on, until one deep flounce falls complete over the other eight. It is said that upon the petticoats worn by the Empress each of these flounces is hemstitched like a pocket-handkerchief, and the outer one, in addition, is nearly covered by embroidery. The effect of this skirt, underneath a ball-dress, or thin dress of any kind, is so charming as to call forth a torrent of the most flattering adjectives of which the French language is capable. We do not anticipate that this Petticoat will become very popular in the United States, as it must necessarily be as expensive as several ordinary skirts, and would seem to require a French blanchisse use to do it up.

We think, therefore, that hoops are likely to reign for some time. Among the best hoop skirts are Madame Demorest's, which are very light and pliable. The steels are very close together, and are connected by cords which do not slip, this being the ordinary fault of hoopskirts.

The jewelry of the 1860s and '70s is best described as heavy, massive, and solid. Massiveness was equated with well made and sturdy. The bigger a piece of furniture or jewelry, surely the better it must be. Colors were also visually heavy. Rich red velvets covered not only furniture and windows, but also "maladies" as well. The feeling of opulence was everywhere.

The most outstanding (pardon the pun) feature of fashion was the hoop skirt, said to have been introduced by Princess Eugenie in Paris. It was not unusual to use as many as 30 yards of material for one skirt. Still, they did tend to make the waist appear smaller, and small waists were definitely in fashion. Laced corsets were also used to minimize the waist. Some ladies wore their lacings so tight they were subject to fainting spells. To further emphasize the waist, buckles came into favor. "Buckles for waist bands have now attained colossal proportions, but these are generally imitation, and not genuine gold and silver..." *Peterson's Magazine* from November 1864 went on to say, "The chased buckles are more distinguished than the plain dead ones, as the workmanship adds to their beauty. The mother-of-pearl buckles are worn with white dresses; and it is fashionable to wear a buckle both at the front and back of the waist."

Godey's Lady's Book, January 1865

General remarks—an English correspondent says: 'Three things in a lady's toilet are now considered necessary, and to appear without them is to appear unfashionable, and these three are—a small bonnet, a wide waistband, and a coat-shaped sleeve.' If the coat basque is worn, the waistband is usually worn over it, but this is so ugly a fashion that we hope it will not last long. The belts are now four to six inches in width, and, of course, the buckles are in proportion. Jet, gilt and jet, plain gilt, steel, and mother-of-pearl buckles are all worn; but the latter is only fashionable for evening wear.

Large buttons 'are all the rage,' the square mother-of-pearl ones being the most handsome, but jet, steel, and gilt are equally worn.

Godey's Lady's Book, 1865

Beads enter largely into the decorations of the present day, and when artistically mounted, are really very effective and beautiful. Some are quite costly, being of malachite, pink or red coral, amber and frosty-looking crystal. All these are employed for head dresses, particularly for the trimming of nets. The invisible nets, which are now woven as fine as hair, are not generally trimmed. The more showy and elaborate kinds form the most effective of coiffures. They are generally very large, and adorned with immense pearl, jet, steel, or crystal beads. The most elegant have a double row of beads forming a coronet in front, while a fringe of beads with pendant ends falls at the back.

Another pretty novelty is the velvet jewelry. These comprise necklaces, bracelets, earrings, buckles, and combs, formed of balls, chains, and grelots of blue or scarlet or black velvet, caught and fastened with gilt and pearl ornaments. This velvet jewelry is extremely pretty and effective with a white dress, and very suitable for a young lady.

A Drawing Room Reception— Godey's Lady's Book, 1865

With Queen Victoria in mourning, her daughters assumed the responsibility of hosting the drawing room receptions. An 1865 issue of *Godey's* had this to say about a recent one:

The Princess Helena of England held a Drawing-Room Reception on the part of her mother. We annex a description of some of the dresses:—

The costume of the Princess was most exquisite: the effect of the lace and tulle both as a trimming and as a skirt to the dress was particularly light and graceful. It may be more accurately described than it is in the official account, by stating that it was composed of rich blue poult de sole, with silver and blonde insertion in squares with ruches; the petticoat being of white glacé trimmed with blue asters; and a tunic of tulle, spotted with silver and finished with silver cord. We may also more correctly add that the Princess Louisa wore a train of rich pink poult de sole, trimmed with crape lesse, pink and white roses, shaded with ferns. The Princess was supported by the Duchess of Wellington, the Queen's mistress of the robes, who wore a silver-like lace over the skirt, which was in keeping, and a sweeping and majestic train of white satin, the noble effect being enhanced by the truly fine display of jewelry. The Princess was surrounded by the royal family; when she was in the front of the throne by her side was the Prince of Wales, and the Princess Mary, of Cambridge, stood with the royal group. Her Royal Highness wore a magnificent and becoming costume de cour, consisting of white satin profusely trimmed with point lace, and displayed some remarkably fine jewelry. The diplomatic corps, with the exception of the Russian Ambassador, were all present.

The display of costumes was chiefly of white, and the taste of the fair wearers, and those who had the difficult task of creating novelty out of the sameness of material, was confined to change of trimming and to the alteration of colors in the skirt. The trains were of a magnitude, which was even astounding to those who have for years wondered when it would end as it came in by slow installments. Happily the arrangements are now excellent, and, considering all things, there is little crushing to be complained of. It certainly has a grand and majestic appearance to see those sweeping trains if they are managed to perfection; but though anxious to be complimentary; we confess that the desired end was not always obtained. The costume of Lady Rendleshand, as regards the elegance of the trimming, was very pretty. Lady Rawlinson wore a splendid rich black velvet costume de cour, on which great taste had been lavished as regards the style of trimming. The costume of Lady Dashwood, whose diamonds were so much admired, was in the best taste, being composed of chené antique silk, with amethyst train and trimming. The display of lace of a rare character was almost remarkable as the display of jewels, the lace worn by the Countess of Portsmouth, Miss F. Noel Mundy, Lady Vivian, Lady Caroline Burgess, and the Marchioness of Ormondo being particularly noticed.

The Jewelry

The display of precious stones seems to become each Drawing Room more remarkable for the extent and costliness. The wearers are no longer satisfied with a few simple decorations, but shower upon themselves, Canae fashion, a very rain of jewels; and at one spot on Thursday, where the light shone especially strong, the wearers seemed to leave a ripple of jeweled prismatic rays on the fair surface. It would be impossible to mention all, but the Duchess of Roxburghe was certainly noticeable for the splendid display of jewels which she wore, consisting chiefly of diamonds of great size and luster. Lady Edith Anbey Hastings wore, in addition to a very tasteful and gorgeous display of jewels, the graceful novelty of diamond epaulettes. Lady Isabella Schuster's diamonds were extremely magnificent. Mrs. Elwon wore a very graceful costume of blue, which was made up so as to introduce in various effects a vast amount of pearls and diamonds, the lace and trimmings being semé with these precious stone. Mrs. Perry Watlington wore a complete set of most magnificent brilliants. The diamonds of Mrs. Rapp were very rich, and the ornaments profuse. The extremely graceful costume of Lady Poltimore was quaintly ornamented with imitation foreign insects. Her Ladyship wore some unique jewels, which were greatly admired; Lady Dashwood's parure of diamonds, the Marchioness of Abbercorn's sapphires and diamonds, and the emeralds and diamonds of Lady Wilton, which were all very beautiful, sufficiently bear out our remark, without further quotation, that the display of jewelry was particularly splendid. The dresses were no less graceful; and it has been agreed by those who have witnessed the Drawing-Rooms for years past, that Thursday's had one of the most distingué assemblages of company and the best dressed witnessed for a long time past. The Countess of Home's costume—the skirt of which was embroidered with steel, the fashionable ornament of the day, was particularly effective.

Changing Fashions

Though *Godey's Lady's Book* was known for its beautifully colored fashion plates, not every department was pleased with women's styles. In 1855, Dr. Jno. Stainback Wilson, editor of the magazine's "Health Department," wrote:

*While we are no Bloomerite, we must enter our
protest against the very long dresses of the present
day. They are cumbersome, uncleanly, and
wastefully extravagant. They prevent freedom of
motion in walking; they gather the dirt from the
roads and streets as they drag their beautiful lengths
along; and they cannot possible last. In view of
all these things, then, and others that might be
mentioned, our verdict is: let the skirts of dresses
be sufficiently bloomerized to swing clear of the
ground, at any rate. Pointed waists are nearly as
bad as corsets. They compress and paralyze the
muscles beneath them; while the internal organs, the
stomach, liver, spleen, etc. are crowded downward,
thus causing a train of most common and serious
disorders to which women are subject.*

The Absurdities of Fashion.

Cartoonists made fun of what they referred to as "The
Absurdities of Fashions." This cartoon, titled "What We May
Expect In The Way of Street Costumes," appeared in the
May 1871 issue of Ballou's Magazine.

In the 1860s, the war helped prove to women just
how impractical their clothes were. When one had to get
up each morning and ride the omnibus to work, it was
painfully apparent that huge hoops had no place on public
transportation. The skirts were also much too long. They
were a nuisance when walking on muddy streets, which
every working woman had to do on occasion. Finally
the fashion experts agreed with Dr. Wilson, even if their
reasons were not the same as his.

By 1874 women were holding dress reform meetings.
Something had to be done. By the 1870s the hoops were
gone, but they were replaced by the bustle. The skirts
were much narrower, but the bustle did protrude. Many
women wanted to do away with this contraption. In April
1887, the fashion editor of the Young Ladies' Journal
wrote, "We are told by competent authorities that steel
tournures, and all the metallic appliances which are so
uncomfortable, are going out of fashion."

Later that same year the writer made this comment:

*Fashion is really becoming quite rational, after all
the extravagances and eccentricities with which has
too justly been charged. It has now become quite
quiet and reasonable.*

*The ridiculous tournures, enormously protruding,
which vexed seriously inclined spirits for the last
few years are now almost forgotten; they have
been transformed into a modest cushion, scarcely
apparent, which offers a timid support to the skirt,
making the bend of the waist. Our shoes and boots,
with stilt-like heels, have long been exchanged for
rational chaussures with low square heels; an absurd
peak by which they terminated hurt so many feet
that it has been found quite necessary to change it
for a rational shape, neither square nor pointed, but
something between the two, which looks graceful
without being uncomfortable. What else were we
blamed for? Extravagant chapeaux, which towered
high above the head (inconvenient hats), which at
the theater played the troublesome part of screens for
these spectators who were unfortunate enough to sit
behind them. Well here reason is triumphant, and
our capotes are perfectly charming; small and well
posed upon the head, they form a most becoming
frame to the face. What, therefore, can modern
Fashion be accused of now? It is quite rational and
practical and logical as most things are in the "Age of
Realism."*

By the end of the decade, the hoops and bustles were gone, but the new "figure showing" fashions still required the structure provided by a body-shaping type of girdle. These would still be too uncomfortable for today's standards.

The Jewelry

We have already explored the jewelry from the 1862 Exhibition in England. Now let's look at some of the jewelry styles of the 1860-'80s time period.

No. 844—$30 per pair.

Our No. 846—$12 per pair.   No. 845—$7 50 per pair.   No. 847—$5 per pair.

No.		Pair.
848	Plain and Chased, all sizes, with guard chains. Pair in case	$2 00
849	Plain and enameled, " " " " "	2 50
850	Plain and chased, child's sizes only, with guard chains. Pair in case.	2 00
851	Plain and enameled, " " " " "	2 50
852	Full enameled, all sizes, with guard chains. Pairs in case	3 00
853	Full enameled, " " " " "	5 00
854	Full enameled, " " " " "	7 50
855	Half enameled, half chased, 5–16 in. wide, in case as above	5 00
856	" " " " 7–16 " " " "	6 00
857	" " " " 9–16 " " " "	8 00
858	" " " " 10–16 " " " "	10 00
859	Half enameled, half chased, Buckle 5–16 in. wide, in case as above..	6 50
860	" " " " 7–16 " " " "	8 00
861	" " " " 9–16 " " " "	10 00
862	" " " " 12–16 " " " "	12 00
863	Roman Gold Buckle, 3–8 in. wide, in case as above.	3 00
864	" " " " 4–8 " " " "	3 50
865	" " " " 6–8 " " " "	4 00
866	Full enameled, finest quality, 5–8 in. wide, in case as above	15 00
867	Handsomely chased and enameled, finest quality 1 in. wide,	20 00
Electro and Fire Gilt Bracelets from 75 cents to $18 00 der dozen pairs.		

These bracelets from an undated Altchul, Seller & Co. catalog are typical of the 1870s. The catalog is likely dated sometime between 1875 and 1889. The prices listed are wholesale. These bracelets are all embellished with taille d'epergne enamel. Some had the enamel on the front half and were chased on the back side.

Toys, Fancy Goods, Etc.   89

BRACELETS.
CELULLOID CORAL.

No. 838—$4 50 per doz. Bell, Shell or Grape Ornaments.

No. 839—$4 00 per doz.

No. 841. $6 per doz.
840, larger, $9 per doz.

No. 842
$2 50 per dozen.

No.		Dozen.
826	Plain narrow Band	$1 50
827	Plain narrow Band with shell or bell bangles.	4 50
828	Single Row Oblong Beads, misses' sizes.	4 50
829	Double Row Oblong Beads, ladies' sizes:	6 00
830	3 Flat Bars	6 00
831	4 Flat Bars	7 00
832	4 Row Snake Coil.	4 50
833	5 Row Snake Coil.	6 00
834	4 Row Snake Coil, ball end	7 50
835	5 Row Snake Coil, with serpent's head.	6 00
836	Flat Cut Bars on elastic	7 50
837	Coil, with rosette and leaf centre.	4 00

All the popular stones of the time were imitated in less expensive materials. These bracelets were advertised as celluloid coral. Note bracelet #842 is made in the crossover design that was so popular in the 1890s-1910. It's interesting to note that the four-row snake coil with ball end bracelet was one of the most expensive designs. The listed prices are per dozen wholesale.

BLACK BRACELETS.
Our stock comprises all the newest styles of black goods, in Horn, Rubber, Imitation Jet, and real Whitby Jet. The patterns are very desirable, and sell readily. These goods range in price per dozen pair:

Horn. . . . .$ 75 to $ 2 25
Rubber. . . . .   2 00 to   8 50
Imitation Jet. . . . . .   8 50 to 15 00
Whitby Jet per pair 1 75 to 10 00

Black bracelets were popular, but the one illustrated here is light in scale and less fancy in design than those from the 1860s. Keep in mind this was a company dealing in less expensive goods that usually reflected the tastes of the working class. The bracelet here is priced by the dozen, except for those made of genuine Whitby jet, which are priced by the pair.

Revivals Continue

By 1864 jewelry designs inspired by earlier finds had spread to the United States. The June issue of *Peterson's Magazine* noted, "The new models are all copied from the antique and give one a very good idea of the beautiful gold and jewel ornaments of Old Grecian Art."

The same publication made this comment in the November issue: "Earrings are now made in the antique style. They represent a large circle, in the center of which either a large ball of dead gold, or five crescents of pearls is fastened; the crescents diminish in size as they ascend. Sometimes the earring is composed of a large crescent of dead gold studded with coral and fringed with gold."

Figs. 6 and 7.—Fashionable styles of earrings.

Fig. 6.   Fig. 7.

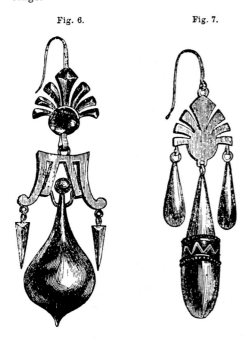

Fig. 6 is of dead gold, with pendants of rock crystal.

Fig. 7 is made of gold and coral, clasped with a fancy band of enamel.

Earrings from Godey's Lady's Book: *"Figures '6' & '7' Fashionable styles of earrings. Figure '6' is of dead gold, with pendants of rock crystal. Figure '7' is made of gold and coral, clasped with a fancy band of enamel."*

Earrings remained an important fashion accessory throughout this time period, as they are today. These two ladies are wearing theirs with pride.

This woman is obviously a lady of the stage wearing a beautiful archaeological-inspired pair of earrings.

Interest in archaeological findings continued to increase. The "Treasure of Priam" was discovered by Heinrich Schlieman in 1869. In 1872 the British Museum bought some fine examples of ancient jewelry from the Castellani Collection. This enabled the British to study and admire the archaeological styles. The French could satisfy their curiosity by viewing the Cavalier Company Collection at the Louvre, and the Italians could study pieces by Augusto Castellani in the Capitone Museum.

In the early 1870s, Luigi P. do Cesnola, a United States consul at Larmoce, discovered the treasure vaults of the Temple of Kurium. An account of the discovery was published in July 1872 in *Harper's New Monthly Magazine*. It was not until 1877 that people in the United States could boast of a collection of archeological finds.

Within the next five years, more discoveries were made on the island of Cyprus. In July 1877, *Harper's* published another article in which they rejoiced at these findings being displayed in the United States: "The Metropolitan Museum of Art had the wisdom to commence its collection of illustrations of ancient at the very beginning of all art, and to offer to its visitors and the American public facilities for studying what no European collection illustrates—the birth of art among civilized men, and its growth in the early years."

Harper's went on to say, "The treasure vaults of Kurium were vast. Gold, silver, alabaster, and bronze, the work of artists and artisans dead more than twenty-five centuries ago, are here gathered; not a few specimens, a ring or two and a gem or two, but literally hundreds of ear and finger rings, bracelets, necklaces, amulets and ornaments in vast variety."

Harper's described many of the pieces, and it had this comment on the earrings: "It cannot fail to strike the observer that the present form was a favorite, and many in this form are evidently Phoenician of an early date. Simple crescents of plain gold are numerous. After these came plain crescents with raised edges and wire ornamentations. Then enamels beautify the crescent. Precious stones are placed on them or form pendants. Then the crescent swells into a solid gold form. Then the hollow gold is shaped in lobes with charming surface ornaments. Then we see agates cut in new-moon form, and set in gold with delicious granulated patterns. There is no end to the varieties of earrings. There are bunches

of fruit, rosettes, plaques with impressed images, earrings with pendants in every form, and earrings with pendants, in the modern form, where a small ornament fits close on the lobe of the ear."

The crescent motif discussed in this article was extremely popular and remained so until after the turn of the century. In the accompanying photos, the dark-haired woman is wearing a crescent brooch that could be set with diamonds or crystals. The other woman shown here is wearing a bigger scale crescent brooch, which may have belonged to her mother or grandmother. Her earrings are circa late 1880s-'90s.

These women are wearing crescent brooches.

The *Harper's* article also gave an excellent description of granulation:

> *This style of work, known in Etruscan jewelry, characterizes much of this ancient Greek work, and is a puzzle to modern goldsmiths. We illustrate a gold ornaments round brooch or amulet—for the sake of describing this remarkable style of work. The surface of this object presents to the eye the appearance of a gold disk stamped in a die, or crossed by numerous fine wires at right angles with each other. On examining it with the magnifying glass, however, it is found that the effect is produced by minute globes of gold, each one perfectly round and smooth, soldered on the surface in exact lines, each globe touching the next. There are on the surface of this small object, a little over an inch in diameter, upward of nine hundred of these globes. How were they made, and how were they soldered on in such absolutely true*

lines? The ablest gold-workers in America (and that is to say the ablest in the world) tell us that they cannot explain it.

Revival jewelry was already in fashion by the time the Metropolitan Museum acquired Cesnola's finds. The *Harper's* article stated:

> *There are some things here in silver which, were they perfect, would ravish the eyes of our lady readers, and over which some of them who love old art will bend in delighted rapture. These are silver belts worn by the ladies of Cyprus in the ancient years. Within the past year or two, a fashion has prevailed among ladies in America of wearing broad metallic belts of silver or other metal. Could an American lady possess one of these belts of Cypriot made in its original freshness, or its facsimile, she would be very happy.*

Ten years later, in 1887, ancient-style jewelry was still being worn. But instead of being made of gold, the designs were now executed in silver. This is confirmed by an article in the *Young Ladies Journal* of January 1887: "Jewels of old silver, finely wrought in the imitation of Ancient jewelry, are also among the favorite trinkets of fashion just now. There are beautiful bracelets composed of detached ovals, fastened together by very fine chains, brooches to match and exquisite chatelaines of the most beautiful workmanship."

As you may have noticed in the previous pages, the name Castellani was mentioned more than once. Even this short history of ancient revivals would not be complete without some mention of this family of famous jewelry artists.

Fortunato Pio Castellani was an excellent Italian craftsman who became interested in Etruscan jewelry while working in an advisory capacity to the Papal government in 1836. This fascination led him to a remote mountain village where workers still used this skill. He persuaded them to come to Rome, and from them he learned this technique. Please note that a definition of granulation is included in the 1877 article in *Harper's*, in which it says, "The ablest gold-workers in America (and that is to say the ablest in the world) tell us that they cannot explain it." Maybe the Americans did not know

how it was done, but the Castellani family became famous with their wonderful copies of the ancient work.

Later Fortunato turned the business over to his sons, Alessandro and Agusto. They also became famous designers.

Another important name in Italian Revivalist jewelry is Giacinto Melillo, who was the manager of Alessandro's workshop before going into business for himself. Another family that became famous in Revival style jewelry was the Giuliano family. For more information on this interesting subject, read *Castellani and Giuliano, Revivalist Jewellers of the 17th Century* by Geoffrey C. Munn.

1887 Jubilee Celebration

Jubilee day was June 21, 1887, but celebrations were held throughout the year. This short description of the occasion gives an idea of the sentiments of the day:

> *There had been other royal jubilees in the history of Great Britain, but none had surpassed that of the year 1887, when the whole land, together with the distant colonies and every quarter of the globe where the British flag waves, rang with the voice of jubilation that the great woman who had ennobled the crown was spared in health and strength to celebrate the fiftieth year of her reign. It was a thrilling moment when, in the blaze of the glorious June sunshine, the Queen drove out through the gates of Buckingham Palace on her way to Westminster Abbey, just as she had done fifty years before on her coronation day. But the bright young girl was now a gray-haired woman who had seen much sorrow and battled with many difficulties. Still, there was a gleam of triumph in her face, for were there not sons and daughters, grandchildren and great-grandchildren rising up to call her blessed, while the shouts of the multitudes which rent the air testified that throughout these fifty years she had retained the love and loyalty of her people.*

> *Jubilee Day, the 21st of June, was a day ever to be remembered by those who were privileged to be in London, and to witness the royal progress*

to Westminster Abbey. The day was observed as a national holiday, and fortunately was one of perfect sunshine. Houses and streets were profusely decorated, and the demonstrations of personal affection for the Queen were universal. Tens of thousands of persons lined the thoroughfares, especially along Piccadilly, Pall Mall, Whitehall, and Parliament Street. The gorgeous cavalcade excited intense interest; the brilliant group consisting of the Prince of Wales, the Crown Prince of Germany, and the Crown Prince of Austria, being singled out for special admiration. [2]

Of course the public wanted souvenirs of the event, and vendors were more than happy to fill this need. Many items added the word "jubilee" to their product as an extra enticement to buy. There was even a "Jubilee Rug Machine" for use in the home. In May of that year, J. Theobald and Company advertised a "Grand Jubilee Prize Picture Puzzle Contest." To enter this competition, one had only to purchase one of the Grand Jubilee Packets "...which have been specially prepared in celebration of Her Majesty's Jubilee. This Packet contains the most marvelous value for the money, as we have determined to make it the most successful that we have ever offered. Everyone who has seen it wonders how we can possibly sell it at the price. As these articles are specially Jubilee goods, every loyal patriotic person ought to possess a parcel, and treasure up the articles as mementos of this most auspicious occasion."[3]

How could any loyal subject resist that offer? The packet contained "The Queen's Jubilee Album" and "... an elegant Jubilee Brooch being a beautiful heavily gold-plated brooch in the shape of an extended fan, with the word 'Jubilee' across it; this is no common loud cheap jewelry, but finished in the highest style of art, and could not be detected from a brooch costing a guinea."

Also included in the package was a "Jubilee fancy scarf pin, most richly finished, the center of the pin represents the Royal Arms of England in brilliant colors, surrounded by a gold-plated band bearing the motto 'Honi qui mal y Pense,' surmounted with the Royal Crown in gold and crimson colours and crossed by two scepters; besides this also a handsome Jubilee Medal bearing the queen's head as a medallion, and the words 'Queen Victoria's Jubilee, 1887' set in a handsome star."

This photograph of Queen Victoria was taken in her 1887 Jubilee Year. It's apparent that she still loves jewelry. Notice that she wears two necklaces, a brooch, and four rings on the one visible hand.

The Queen in her State Robes (1887) from the photograph by Walery, Regent Street. Note the necklace and earrings the queen is wearing. The necklace contains 25 cushion-shaped diamonds set in silver with gold links. The center diamond drop is set in platinum and weighs 22.48 cts. It was originally known as the Lahore diamond. Each of the nine larger stones weighs between 11.25 and 8.25 cts. The drop pendants on the earrings alone weigh approximately 19 cts. As you can see, the diamond weight alone is well over 100 cts.

A Silver Jubilee brooch owned by the author. $175.

A gold commemorative of the Silver Jubilee event, embellished with rubies and one sapphire. Note that the brooch has the shape and outline of the garter.

Diamonds

In the coverage of the 1862 exposition, the amount of diamonds used in jewelry was phenomenal. It is only natural to wonder where they all came from.

The early diamonds came from India and Borneo. The Koh-i-Noor (Mountain of Light) came from India. It was originally a round stone weighing 186 carats but it was recut to weigh 108.2 carats. This stone was on display at the 1862 Exhibition with permission from its owner, the queen. As you may remember from the previous drawing room reception article, the queen often wore the Koh-i-Norr diamond as a brooch.

In the first quarter of the 18th century, diamonds were discovered in the region of Minas Gerais in Brazil. In 1867 diamonds were discovered in South Africa. A peasant boy playing near a river found a pretty stone and took it home. A traveler passing through the village saw the boy's prize and suspected what it might be. He was right; it was a diamond valued at $2,500. Word of the find spread, and the diamond rush began. Within a few years, wearing diamonds was even more in style, and this new source was supplying the Paris demand.

Diamonds have always been coveted. The Greeks appreciated the stone's hardness and called it "Adamas," meaning "unconquerable." Consequently, it was often worn into battle. The stones were not cut or faceted as they are today, but worn in their natural pointed shape. These early diamonds were found in the streams of India. These alluvial diamonds required no mining because the natural erosion of the earth uncovered them. Until 1871, alluvial diamonds were the only ones available to man.

By chance it was discovered that diamonds were buried deep inside the earth in what are now known as pipes. These pipes are thought to be part of extinct volcanoes. A most famous pipe in South Africa, known as the Kimberly mine, was worked from 1871 until after the turn of the century. The rock surrounding the diamond is called blue ground. It is estimated that an average of two tons of blue ground must be mined to find a single carat of diamonds.

Diamonds are judged by carat weight, cut, clarity, and color. Consequently, three stones each weighing one carat could vary thousands of dollars in price. A carat weighs 200 milligrams, which is equal to 100 points. Hence, a half-carat is 50 points, and a fourth of a carat equals 25 points.

The cut of a diamond is very important. It takes an expert to decide the proper cut for each stone. The proper proportions enhance the stone's brilliance and increase its value. Most diamonds today are brilliant cut and have 58 facets. Most diamonds in the Victorian era were cut in what is known as old mine-cut.

The clarity of a diamond is determined by the purity of the stone. Flaws such as dark inclusions and feathers can greatly decrease the value. A diamond is considered to be flawless if there are no visible flaws when the stone is examined using a 10 power loupe.

Diamonds come in a variety of colors. Some are colorless, many have a yellowish tinge, and a few have a bluish tinge. When fancy colors such as green, violet, brown, blue, red, and yellow are found in quality stones, they are very expensive and highly collectible. Since diamonds tend to pick up color from surrounding objects, a white background is best when determining a stone's true color.

Because the diamond has always been highly prized, there have been many imitations. These include rock crystal, zircon, spinel, white sapphire, and glass.

Opals

In 1870 a huge opal field was discovered in Australia. This prompted Queen Victoria to try again to lift the veil of superstition that had befallen the stone. The novel, Anne of Geierstein, written by Sir Walter Scott and published in 1829, was responsible for the opal being considered bad luck. Lady Heroine, a character in the book, always wore an opal in her hair. Its iridescent glow seemed to reflect her every mood. When she came to a tragic end, the opal's mysterious powers were blamed.

The opal was one of Queen Victoria's favorite stones. She gave them as wedding gifts to her daughters and wore them herself. Still, the superstition remained. When Napoleon presented the Empress Eugenie with a parure of opals, she refused them. Even today some people think it is unlucky to wear an opal unless it is a birthstone. Others believe, as the ancients did, that the stone brings good fortune to its wearer.

In spite of the people who didn't want an opal, there were many who still chose to wear what they referred to as the "magic stone." Many were shown with pride at the 1862 Exhibition. By the end of the century, opals were one of the most fashionable stones.

There are three types of opals: precious, fire, and common. The precious is the kind most people associate with the word "opal." It has a beautiful multicolored iridescence that changes when exposed to different angles of light. The most common color of precious opal is white. There are also black opals, but they are very rare. Opals may also be found in gray, blue, or green.

The fire opal is named for its orange color. It is not opalescent, and it does not have the rainbow-like colors. The best of this type are clear and transparent. Another variety of the fire opal is the Mexican water opal. It is

usually light brown or colorless. The so-called common opals are varied. There are agate opals, wood opals, honey opals, milk opals, and moss opals. The average person would never identify most of these as opals.

Because opals are as much as 30 percent water, they require very special treatment. If a stone gets too dry, it tends to crack or lose its iridescent quality. In the book Gemstones of the World, Walter Schumann suggests the best treatment is to "...saturate the stone with oil or water and to avoid the aging process by storing the piece in moist absorbent cotton."

By 1886 opals had lost their unearned reputation for being unlucky and were being used in the newest designs. "During the last few years, a reaction has taken place and American women are accepting the magic gem," an article in the August 1886 edition of Godey's Lady's Book reported. "Many superb designs are seen at the jewelers, one of the latest being a golden eagle with outstretched wings, thickly studded with opals, the edges being encrusted with tiny scintillant diamonds. The shimmering changeful fire of the opal renders it suitable for articles of jewelry to be worn in the evenings, the light glinting upon the translucent hues of the lovely gem in a most fascinating manner. There are striking designs of butterflies, dragonflies and beetles, in opals associated with emeralds and diamonds. These stones admirably express the brilliant beauty of the insects."

A love token necklace in a heart motif is set with a beautiful opal surrounded by diamonds.

Garnets

The strong color of the garnet was favored by the Victorians. It was beautiful faceted or cut en cabochon. The word "garnet" came from a word meaning glowing coals and usually conjures up pictures of a wine red stone. Actually, garnets can be found in every color except blue. This group of stones has the same structure but differs chemically.

Garnets most often associated with the names almandine (AL-man-dine) and pyrope (PIE-rope) are also the most common.

Pyrope garnets were popular during 1860-1889. Their deep, rich color was a favorite accessory for the massive clothing of the 1860s and '70s. Bohemian garnets, fashioned in lighter-scale mountings, continued to be popular in the 1880s and '90s. They are red or reddish brown in color and tend to be more transparent than the almandine garnet. Most pyrope garnets are mined in Czechoslovakia, Australia, and South Africa.

The almandine garnet tends to have a slightly purplish tint. The most common variety of garnet, it is found in Brazil, India, Australia, Czechoslovakia, and Sri Lanka.

The garnet is the accepted January birthstone. Some believe that it empowers the wearer with truth, constancy, and faith. Ancient man wore it for protection against being struck by lightning. No matter the reason for wearing them, garnets always seem to be admired and enjoyed, especially when set in Victorian jewelry.

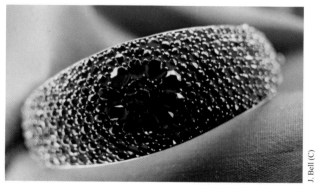

Bracelet pavé set with garnets that cover the entire piece. This is the color that we normally associate with garnets, although they come in every color except blue.

Amethyst

The amethyst is a member of the quartz family of stones. It is known for its violet to red-purple hue. In fact, the name amethyst is now synonymous with the color. The finest colored and most valuable are known as Siberian amethysts. This refers to the quality of the stone and not the location from which it comes.

The amethyst was a very fashionable stone throughout the Victorian era. Because of its ecclesiastical association, it was acceptable to wear in the latter stages of mourning. Since amethysts were plentiful, they were affordable and could be worn by all classes. In a yellow gold or pinchbeck mounting, surrounded by seed pearls, they were quite lovely.

In olden days, the amethyst was believed to possess the power to protect the wearer and bring good luck. The people born in February are fortunate to be able to claim this as their birthstone.

This ring in 14k yellow gold is set with an amethyst embellished with an incised flower motif inlaid with beaten gold and set with a diamond.

Jet

Jet, a hard, coal-like material, is a type of fossilized wood. The finest jet was mined in the town of Whitby, England. The jet industry started there in the early 19th century, and by 1850, there were 50 jet workshops. Because it lent itself well to carving and kept a sharp edge, it was used extensively. By 1873, there were more than 200 jet shops in this one small town.

Jet was a popular material for mourning jewelry long before the death of Queen Victoria's beloved husband. In fact, Victoria had worn jet jewelry while in mourning for her Uncle King, William IV. At the time of Albert's death, she was still in mourning for her mother, who had died in March 1861.

Albert's unexpected death left the English subjects shocked and grieved. The entire nation went into mourning. Americans also had many reasons to mourn. The Civil War took its toll, and almost every family in the North and South was touched by the hand of death. Then in 1865 President Lincoln was assassinated. Jet was an obvious solution to the problem of what jewelry would be suitable during this period of grief.

Because jet is extremely lightweight, it was the perfect material for making the enormous lockets, necklaces, brooches, and bracelets that were so popular in the 1860s and 1870s. The success enjoyed by jet factories led to many imitations. French jet, which is neither French nor jet (it is actually black glass), was cheaper to manufacture. It gave the jet industry some competition, but because it is much heavier, it was used in the making of beads and smaller items. Other materials used to imitate jet were dyed horn, gutta-percha, bog oak, and onyx.

Although jet was worn for mourning, it was not used only for that purpose. Polished jet beads, cameos, bracelets, and earrings did not have to be put away when the mourning period was over. Jet became fashionable in and of itself, and was used to make frames and handles for bags and to embellish ball gowns.

The woman in this photograph appears to be wearing a jet necklace and locket.

This woman is wearing a beautiful jet bead necklace.

The jet necklace in the picture on the left is from the author's collection. It looks almost art deco with the triangular embellishments holding the three strands of carved jet, but it is circa 1870-'80s. The jet necklace in the photograph on the right, circa 1875, is in the Victoria and Albert Museum in London. The two are very similar.

Venetian Mosaics

For hundreds of years some of the finest decorative glass in the world has been made in Murano, a tiny island off the coast of Venice. It is amazing to watch the glass blowers at work with the beautiful multicolored rods of glass. They make all types of glass items including paperweights, vases, animals, and utilitarian items such as drinking glasses.

During the 19th century and the early 20th century, mosaics, referred to as Venetian mosaics, were popular. They were used for pins, pendants, bracelets, and also to embellish pieces that were made of other materials.

Motifs were designed out of small pieces of colored glass and multicolored glass rods. They have an entirely different look from the other two types of mosaic. Consequently, they are visually identifiable just as the others are. The earlier pieces are usually much better works than the later ones. As the art declined, the pieces that create the design seem to get larger and are less flushly set than the earlier ones. As with other pieces, construction methods, fittings and findings, and scale help in determining circa dates. Another clue is the colors used in the pieces. They are often a good indicator of date.

Earrings with Venetian mosaic set into goldstone.

Goldstone

Goldstone is an imitation aventurine made of glass to which copper crystals have been added. It has a gold spangled look that is quite attractive. Once seen, it is easy to recognize.

Goldstone is quite often encountered in old jewelry. It is said that it was first made in the 18th century when a glassmaker accidentally dropped some gold colored filings in the glass. Goldstone was used for the ground of

some mosaics and as a stone for cuff links or stickpins. Since it is neither gold nor a stone, it can be added to the list of misnomers in the jewelry field.

Cock Cover Jewelry

In the late 1880s it became popular to take the cock covers from watches from the 1600s and 1700s and use them to make jewelry. The beautiful hand-pierced cocks had been saved by watch repairmen who appreciated their beauty when breaking up old watches for parts and melting down cases.

The cock was a protective cover for the watch's balance wheel and staff. These covers were made by women, young girls, and young boys who worked in this cottage industry. The pierced work designs were beautifully hand-cut. This process sometimes took days or even weeks to complete. Many cocks were decorated with swans, masks, and sometimes even initials.

Victorian ladies who saw these carved and engraved pieces were fascinated with their graceful beauty and urged the watchmakers to sell the pieces, which were then made into necklaces, earrings, and bracelets.

The metal used for these cock covers was almost always gilded brass. The jewelry was made from approximately 1885 through the end of the century. It is the author's theory that the beautiful pierced tracery work we find in platinum jewelry made at the turn of the century was inspired by these pieces.

A watch movement showing the decorative cock cover that protected the important balance and staff of the watch.

Look very closely at the bottom of the cock and notice the engraved face. Some of the pieces have swans in the center and other beautiful motifs. This one has a flower in the center and pierced flowers and foliage.

A simple brooch made from three English cocks. Note the details and the beautiful patterns. The cock on the left has an urn engraved on the foot, and the cock on the right has a basket for the flowers.

Chatelaines

In 1863 Prince Albert, Victoria's firstborn son, married Princess Alexandra, the eldest daughter of the king of Denmark. The country rejoiced with the royal family. They were also delighted to have a young, beautiful new addition to the family, one that they could look to for the newest in fashions. She not only reflected fashions, she also set them.

Chatelaines had gone out of style in the 1860s, but Alexandra revived the fashion by wearing one. In 1887 the *Young Ladies' Journal* felt it necessary to explain to the younger generation what a chatelaine was: "The chatelaine consists of an ornamental hook to fasten to the waistband, from which suspends five chains, each upholding some article necessary to the work-table, for instance, a thimble holder, a pair of scissors made so as to fasten in their points when not wanted, a pincushion and a yard measure. In some models the latter are exchanged for a silver pencil-case, and a scent-bottle, or a tiny notebook, while some ladies prefer a silver whistle or a circle for suspending a bunch of keys."

Metals

Silver

In the 1860s the Comstock Lode was discovered in Virginia City, Nevada. This site was reported to have yielded over $350 million worth of gold and silver. With this new source of silver, plus the amount of silver artifacts found in archeological sites, the metal became more fashionable. Another factor in its acceptance was the emergence of a working force of women. The benefits of the reduced cost of mass-produced items, added to a woman's ability to buy jewelry for herself, created another buying level in the marketplace.

Silver jewelry began to emerge in popularity for women in the 1870s, and by the end of the 1880s it was worn by women of every class. This love for white metal continued into the next century.

Jewelry in Photographs

Please take note of the jewelry worn in the following photographs from the author's collection. Keep in mind that most people who had their pictures taken wore jewelry that they liked, and often it had been in the family for years. The jewelry items worn in these photos are from the 1860-'80s time period. The approximate age of each picture is determined by identifying the jewelry, clothing, and hairstyles. These pictures are shown in the chronological order of the jewelry and not necessarily that of the photo.

Both of these tintypes show women wearing brooches. The woman on the left is wearing a brooch that appears to be made of jet or gutta-percha. The woman on the right is wearing matching cameo earrings and brooch.

This picture shows a woman wearing a matching set of cameo earrings and brooch from the 1870s.

The cameo shown in this photo appears to be made of shell and has the motif of "Leda and the Swan," circa 1860s.

From the mid-1870s until after the turn of the century, horizontal brooches were very much in vogue.

Both of these photos show horizontal bar-style brooches. Notice that the woman on the left has a fringe hairstyle made popular by Princess Alexandra, who was destined to be the British queen in 1901.

This photo shows a horizontal knot brooch.

These two sisters are wearing horizontal brooches. The woman on the right is wearing a brooch similar to the brooch worn by the woman with the fringe hairstyle, above.

Crosses were popular attachments for book chains. This woman is also wearing a cameo brooch.

Each of these women is wearing a book chain with cross and a horizontal brooch at the neck of her dress.

These two babies are wearing sentiment pins.

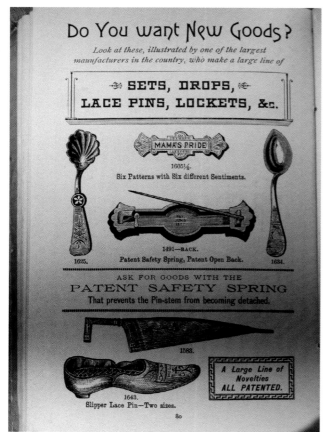

This advertisement from the Jewelers Directory in 1884 illustrates that even babies wore horizontal pins. Notice that the one in the middle has "Mama's Pride," but the advertisement states that they have six patterns with six different sentiments. They were gold-filled and now sell for $125-$150 each.

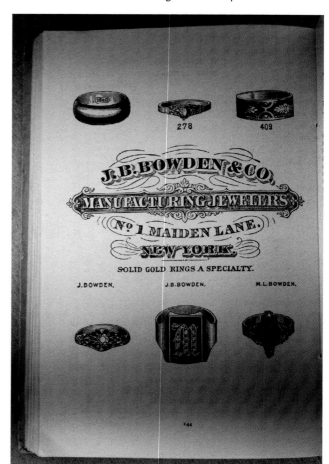

An assortment of rings from the 1884 Jewelers Directory.

 # The Fashions

Here are some fashions taken from women's magazines of the era. *Graham's Magazine, Peterson's Magazine,* and *Godey's Lady's Book* were popular magazines throughout the 19th century. These fashion plates were hand colored and continued to be so throughout the 1880s. Then we will visually explore the jewelry that was used to accessorize these fashions.

Godey's Lady's Book, *February 1860, "How Do I Look?"*

Godey's Lady's Book *fashions for March 1862.*

June 1862 fashions in Godey's Lady's Book.

These Godey's Lady's Book fashions from August 1862 show how important it was for women to be well covered. Unlike today, no woman back then wanted to get sunburned. Ladies had white skin. Only the ones who "worked the fields" got tanned. Today it's just the opposite: Tanned skin indicates a woman who can afford to lounge around in the sun or spend time in a tanning bed. Quite a reversal in fashion.

Godey's Lady's Book from September 1862.

Godey's Lady's Book *from September 1863. Note the bracelets the ladies are wearing.*

October 1863 fashions from Godey's Lady's Book.

Peterson's Magazine *fashions from February 1864. These were listed as "housedresses." Can you imagine wearing one of these around the house every day?*

Godey's Lady's Book *December 1864 fashions.*

Peterson's Magazine, *January 1865.*

Peterson's Magazine, *February 1865.*

Godey's Lady's Book, *May 1865.*

Peterson's Magazine, *July 1866.*

September 1866 Peterson's Magazine.

October 1866 Peterson's Magazine.

Peterson's Magazine, *April 1872.*

Peterson's Magazine, *August 1872.*

January 1874 Peterson's Magazine, *"The Opera Box."*

September 1874 Peterson's Magazine, *"The Autumn Woods."* Obviously, they were just looking at the woods and not intending to go for a walk.

January 1880 Peterson's Magazine, *"The New Year's Reception."* Note that the bustle is no longer protruding to unsightly dimensions.

Peterson's Magazine, *August 1880.*

December 1880 fashions from Peterson's Magazine, *"The Skating Park." Not much bustle, but look at how tightly fitting the bottoms of the dresses have become.*

July 1881 Peterson's Magazine, *"The Garden Party." Notice the smaller scale earrings on the lady in the middle.*

Pricing Section
1860s, '70s, and '80s

Bracelets

Bracelet, circa 1860s, pique links with heart-shaped drop.

Price: $4,545

Courtville Antiques (D)

Sue Brown (D)

Bracelet, circa 1860s, pique bracelet joined by a tortoiseshell heart, squeeze locket to open.

Price: $2,610

Bracelet, circa 1860s, 14k mesh set with amethyst with pearl inset center.

Price: $1,000

Stone Home Antiques (D)

Bracelet, circa 1860s, low k gold, paved with round rose-cut garnets over the entire surface, center has pear-shaped and oval rose-cut garnets in flower motif, 1-3/4" in the center, tapers down to approximately 1" in back.

Price: $1,800

Jeanenne Bell (C)

Bracelet, circa 1860s, sterling silver set with lava cameos in various colors, 1-1/8" x 7/8".

Price: $1,800

Jeanenne Bell (C)

Jewelry Box Antiques (D)

Veritas (D)

Bracelet, circa 1860s, jet segments with elastic, oval center with cut steel star, 1-2/8" x 1-5/8".

Price: $550

Bracelet, circa 1860s, silver mountings with inlaid Scottish stones in a mosaic pattern, embellished with citrines.

Price: $750

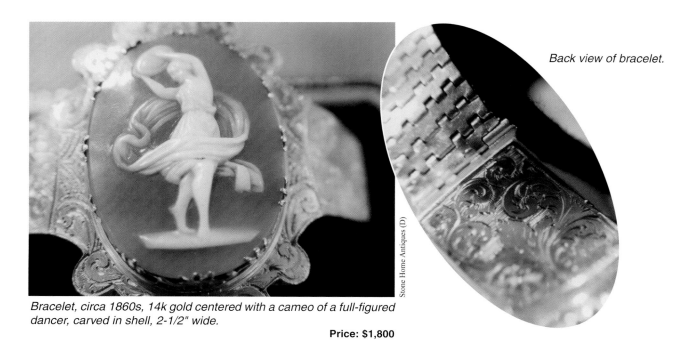

Back view of bracelet.

Bracelet, circa 1860s, 14k gold centered with a cameo of a full-figured dancer, carved in shell, 2-1/2" wide.

Price: $1,800

Bracelet, circa 1860s, 15k gold, wide-hinged bangle, Archeological Revival style,1-3/4" wide, embellished with pearls.

Price: $1,750

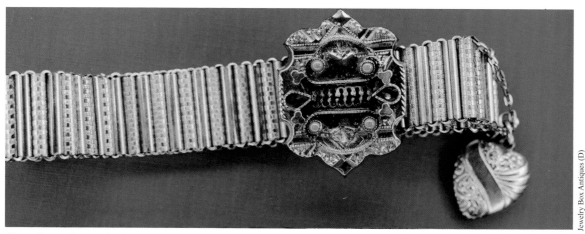

Bracelet, yellow gold-filled slide set with turquoise, attached is a later addition heart drop, 3-1/2".

Price: $375

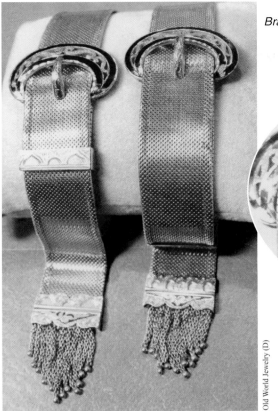

Bracelet, circa 1860-'70s, 14k yellow gold, buckle-style with blue enamel.
Price: $2,200

Old World Jewelry (D)

Close-up of buckle slide.

Stone Home Antiques (D)

Bracelet, circa 1870s, silver set with lava cameos, each segment the size of elongated quarter.
Price: $2,100

Photo courtesy Skinner 3-16-04 (A)

Bracelet, 14k gold mount, antique carnelian agate cameo carved to depict two ladies flanking a classical soldier within foliate scrolling frames completed by a gate link bangle (cameo surrounds stained black for mourning).
Price: $2,350

Old World Jewelry (D)

Bracelet, circa 1870s, 14k gold, 5/8" hinged bangle, buckle motif with black taille d' épergne enamel.

Price: $2,200

Siaren Duncan-August (D)

Pair of bracelets, circa 1870s, 18k gold, matching Venetian mosaic, can be joined together to make a necklace.
Price: $1,200

Close-up of the mosaics.

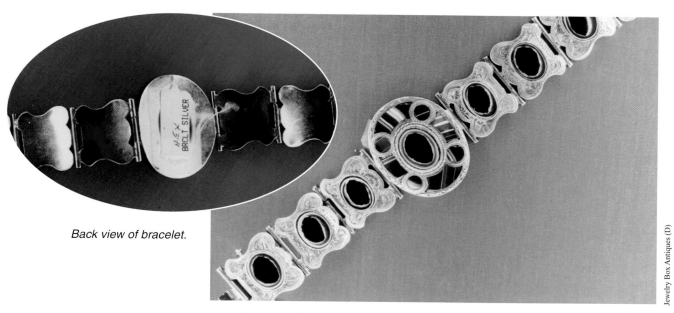

Back view of bracelet.

Bracelet, circa 1870s, sterling silver with cabochon banded agate and inlaid stones, each link approximately 7/8" x 7/8".

Price: $750

Bracelet, hinged bangle, modified buckle motif with turquoise, pearls, and diamonds, 1" wide.

Price: $3,015, £1,675

Bracelet, circa 1870s, coral, made by Phillips of Cockspur.

Price: $8,100, £4,500

Jewelry Box Antiques (D)

Bracelet, gold-filled, 1/2" wide, slide 7/8".
Price: $425

Photo courtesy Skinner 12/9/03 (A)

Bracelet, circa 1870s, 18k gold and lapis bangle, Etruscan Revival, one half set with a curved lapis tablet, the other with delicate bead and wirework motifs.
Price: $3,407

Agan Antiques (D)

Bracelet, circa 1870, bog oak, center disk covered with shamrocks, disks on either side of center plaque set with faceted black stones, other disks are slightly cone-shaped, center plaque 1-1/2" diameter, each side 15/16".
Price: $345

Bracelets, circa 1870-'80s, one with black enamel slide, one with cameo slide.
Price: $400 (smaller), $450

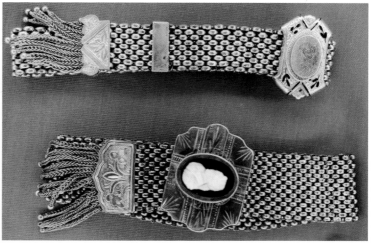

Jewelry Box Antiques (D)

Code by photograph credit line:

(A) Auction House—Auction Price

(C) Collector—Collector Asking Price

(D) Dealer—Dealer Asking Price

Bracelet, circa 1870s, Venetian mosaic, each side has different colors and patterns.

Price: $1,100

Jeanenne Bell (D)

Opposite side of bracelet.

Bracelet, yellow gold-filled with slide centered with a stone cameo.

Price: $400

Jewelry Box Antiques (D)

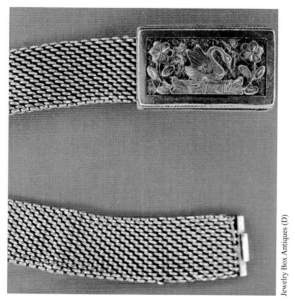

Bracelet, dated July 22, 1884, yellow gold-filled mesh with multi-gold buckle.

Price: $375

Jewelry Box Antiques (D)

Bracelet, circa 1880s, yellow gold-filled, multi-gold.

Price: $249

Jewelry Box Antiques (D)

Bracelet, circa 1880, jet segments strung on elastic, embellished with old-cut rhinestones.

Price: $250

Jewelry Box Antiques (D)

Bracelet, circa 1880s, 18k gold set with sapphires, rubies, and pearls, unusual with the dangling bits on the bracelet.

Price: $2,109, £1,170

Launder Antiques (D)

Bracelet, circa 1880-'90s, 18k gold, bangle with blue enamel and half pearls, four-petal flower.

Price: $3,015, £1,675

Messada Antiques (D)

Photo courtesy Bonhams & Butterfield 12/16/03 (A)

Bracelet, circa 1880, 14k gold, diamond and enamel bangle designed with double hinged central ornament prong-set with a mine-cut diamond weighing approximately 1.40 carats, flanked by two round reliquary compartments, decorated with blue enamel, 6-1/2".

Price: $3,200

Jewelry Box Antiques (D)

Bracelet, circa 1880s, open jet circle, links strung with elastic.

Price: $270

Photo courtesy Sotheby's of London (D)

Bracelet, circa 1880s, bangle set in the center with a cultured pearl measuring approximately 13 mm, border and shoulders set with cushion-shaped, circular, and rose-cut diamonds, diameter approximately 55 mm.

Price: $4,620, £2,400

Old World Jewelry (D)

Bracelet, circa 1880s, 15k hollow gold, love knot, 5/8" wide.

Price: $1,300

Veritas (D)

Bracelet, circa 1880s, Venetian mosaic.

Price: $1,500

Jeanenne Bell (C)

Pair of bracelets, gold, crossover style baby bracelets done in Etruscan Revival style, set with garnets, (one shown).

Price: $800

Bracelet, circa 1880-'90s, 8-9k gold, garnet, big clasp.
Price: $1,800

Jane Fletcher (D)

Back view showing construction.

Bracelet, circa 1880s, 14k yellow gold centered with coral cameo.
Price: $1,100

Stone Home (D)

Back view showing construction.

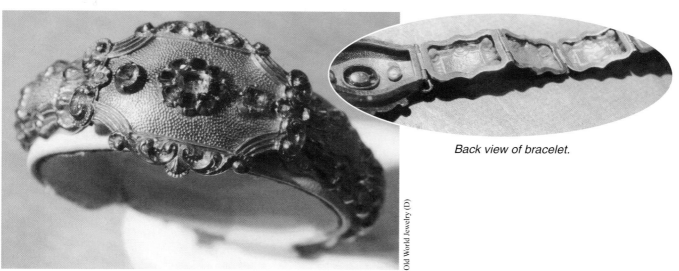

Back view of bracelet.

Old World Jewelry (D)

Bracelet, circa 1880s, 15ct gold, foil back beryl.

Price: $2,250

Old World Jewelry (D)

Bracelet, circa 1880s, 14k gold, hinged bangle, taille d' épergne, enamel and stone cameo.

Price: $1,675

Jewelry Box Antiques (D)

Bracelet, circa 1880, gold over brass, hinged bangle, 2", nicely engraved.

Price: $350

Jewelry Box Antiques (D)

Bracelet, circa 1870-'80s, gold over silver, rams head and mesh, 1/4" x 3/4".

Price: $500

Launder Antiques (D)

Bracelet, circa 1880s, flexible, turquoise buckle motif.

Price: $1,485, £825

Jeanenne Bell (C)

Bracelet, circa 1880s, made from watch cock covers.

Price: $800

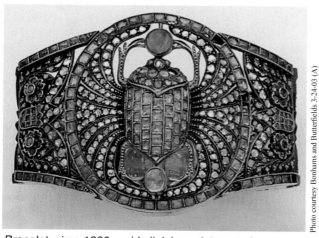

Photo courtesy Bonhams and Butterfields 3-24-03 (A)

Bracelet, circa 1880s, wide link bracelet centering an oval central ornament depicting a beetle set throughout with rectangular-cut emeralds and faceted rose-cut diamonds, accented by rose-cut sapphires and rubies, the front and back legs holding collet-set bullet-shaped emerald cabochons, completed by tapered lotus flower motif links, set with table-cut diamonds, round- and rectangular-cut emeralds, and rose-cut rubies, French assay marks, 6-3/4" long.

Price: $9,400

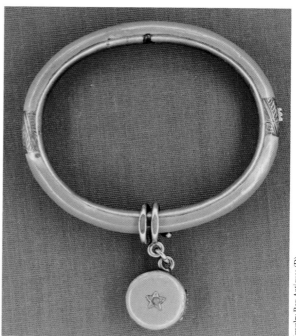

Jewelry Box Antiques (D)

Bracelet, late 1880s-'90s, blue enamel and attached locket set with half pearl, for a small lady or child.

Price: $850

Brooches

Wimpler Antiques (D)

Brooch, circa 1860-'70, silver set with cross in center, bloodstone and red jasper with star burst around the edges, 2".

Price: $711

Wimpler Antiques (D)

Brooch, circa 1860-'70, silver, Scottish, set with three citrines, amethyst, jasper, and agate, 2-1/2" x 2".

Price: $873

Messada Antiques (D)

Brooch, circa 1860s, enamel on copper, 2" wide x 1-3/4" long.

Price: $2,790, £1,550

Back view of brooch showing construction methods.

Brooch, circa 1860-'70s, pique, gold, and silver in a fancy pattern on a round disk, very good condition.
Price: $585, £310

Gold mounting, black and white banded agate encircled with pearls, compartment in back for hair, newer safety clasp.
Price: $5,355, £2,975

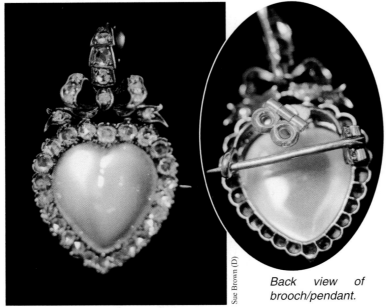

Back view of brooch/pendant.

Brooch/pendant, circa 1860s, gold mounting, diamond and moonstone heart, considered a love token jewel, detachable pendant so both can be worn separately.
Price: $4,049, £2,145

Brooch, circa 1860, 15k gold set with classic shell cameo with lion mask on shoulder.
Price: $1,105, £2,089

Michael Sher (D)

Brooch, circa 1860s, gold mounting set with shell cameo, Egyptian Revival, approximately 4".
Price: $650

Agan Antiques (D)

Brooch, circa 1860s, bog oak souvenir from a visit to Muckross Abbey ruins, 1-1/2" diameter.
Price: $95

Agan Antiques (D)

Brooch/pendant combination, circa 1860s, gutta-percha, deer motif, 2" wide x 2-1/2" long.
Price: $225

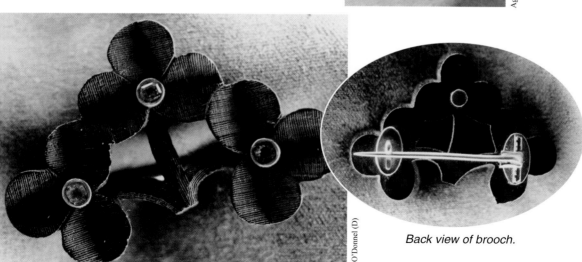

June O'Donnel (D)

Back view of brooch.

Brooch, circa 1860s, yellow gold with bog oak shamrocks, centered with emeralds, 2" x 1-1/2".
Price: $300

Beverly Tarren (D)

Brooch, circa 1860s, rolled gold set with lava cameo in deep relief, revolves so the lava carving or the ivory can be shown, inspired by a mosaic in ruins of Pompeii, 3" x 2-3/4".
Price: $995

Messada Antiques (D)

Brooch, circa 1860s, gold set with pink shell cameo of a lady with deep flowers in her hair.
Price: $2,295, £1,215

Launder Antiques (D)

Brooch, circa 1860s, metal mount set with rare shell cameo, subject is "Flight into Egypt," donkey with Virgin Mary and Baby Jesus on his back, Joseph leading donkey with angel overhead.
Price: $435, £225

Messada Antiques (D)

Brooch, circa 1860s, gold mounting set with amethyst cameo surrounded by pearls, carved in high relief, glazed compartment in back.
Price: $5,355, £2,450

Brooch, circa 1860s, gold mounting set with cabochon and rose-cut garnets, 8 cm x 4-1/2 cm.

Price: $1,224, £680

Charlotte Sayer (D)

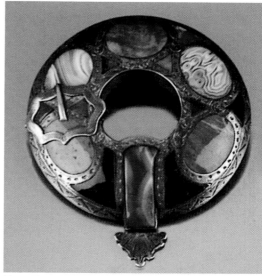

Photo courtesy Skinner, Boston 6/17/03 (A)

Brooch, sterling silver engraved mount set with Scottish agate, designed as a garter buckle.

Price: $676

Photo courtesy Skinner, Boston 6/17/03 (A)

Brooch, sterling silver engraved mount set with Scottish agate, designed with a star centering a circular-cut citrine.

Price: $705

Sue Brown (D)

Brooch, circa 1860s, gold mounting set with large scale scenic shell cameo, from the Naples area.

Price: $2,070, £1,150

Brooch, circa 1860s, Whitby jet cameo carved and signed by John Speedy. Speedy carved cameo portraits for famous people such as Queen Victoria and Charles Dickens. They sat for him as they would a portrait painter. Princess Alexander gave him an award at the Chelsea Art Club, which was enough money to pay off his indenture and set him up in business. At that time he was only 23 years old, so he had many years to produce his work. He tended to sign his pieces in the neck area. This one is signed "J. Speedy" on the ridge that is under the neck.

Value unknown

Brooch, circa 1860, ivory floral motif carved in France for English market.
Price: $200

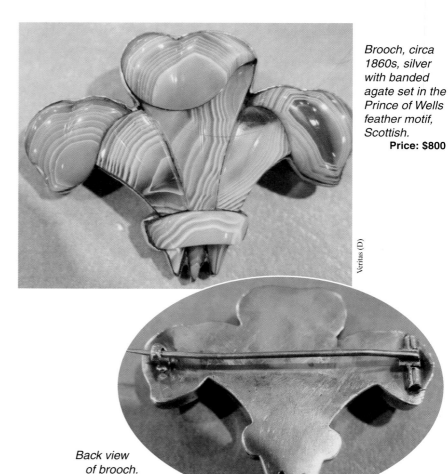

Brooch, circa 1860s, silver with banded agate set in the Prince of Wells feather motif, Scottish.
Price: $800

Back view of brooch.

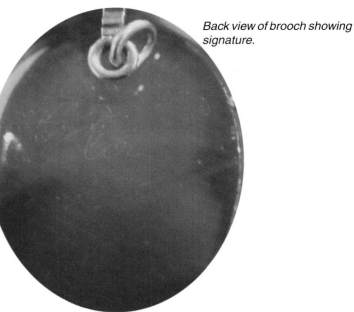

Back view of brooch showing signature.

Brooch/pendant, circa 1860-'80s, gold mounting set with stone cameo with mine-cut diamonds.
Price: $5,000

Stone Home (D)

Old World Jewelry (D)

Brooch, circa 1860s, painting on porcelain, Vagabond Boy, 2-1/2" x 2".
Price: $350

Photo courtesy Skinner 3-16-04 (A)

Brooch, 14k gold, hardstone cameo depicting a classical lady in profile wearing an ivy garland, scrolling frame accented by seed pearls, French guarantee stamp.
Price: $2,703

Two brooches: Left: bog oak, engine-turned border with carved shamrocks, 2-1/2" diameter.

Price: $300

Right: Hand-carved scene of the ruins of Muckross Abbey, 3" x 2-1/2".

Price: $350

Jewelry Box Antiques (D)

Back view showing glass missing from hair compartment.

Revolving brooch, circa 1860-'70s, 18k gold set with stone cameo and embellished with black taille d' épergne enameling.

Price: $2,800

Jeanenne Bell (C)

Brooch, gold over brass, pavé set with rose-cut, round, and pear-shaped garnets, approximately 2-3/4" x 2".

Price: $800

Jewelry Box Antiques (D)

Jewelry Box Antiques (D)

Brooch, circa 1860-'70s, jet cameo, beautifully done.

Price: $375

Messada Antiques (D)

Brooch, circa 1870s, pietre dure, flower motif.

Price: $1,665, £925

Messada Antiques (D)

Brooches, circa 1860-'70s, three-color gold decoration, matching stone cameos, 1" diameter.

Price: $13,770, £7,650

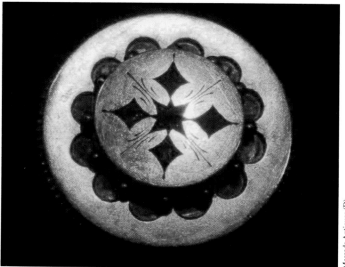

Messada Antiques (D)

Brooch, circa 1870s, rose-cut diamond, compartment in back for a lock of hair, 1-1/4" diameter.

Price: $1,575, £875

Brooch, circa 1860-'70s, 18k gold, pietre dure, white flowers.

Price: $900

Jane Fletcher (D)

Veritas (D)

Brooch, circa 1870s, Scottish, 2-1/2" diameter.

Price: $450

Brooch/pendant, circa 1870-'80s, 18k stone cameo of man with cross, two-color enamel, religious token, glazed compartment in back for hair, 2-1/2".

Price: $3,200

Old World Jewelry (D)

Code by photograph credit line:

(A) Auction House—Auction Price

(C) Collector—Collector Asking Price

(D) Dealer—Dealer Asking Price

Photo courtesy Sotheby's of London 12-16-03 (A)

Brooch, circa 1870s, designed as a textured gold scallop shell, the central blister pearl within lines of cushion-shaped and rose-cut diamonds, two diamonds deficient, velvet scallop-shaped fitted case.

Price: $1,400-1,700, £960

Photo courtesy Bonhams and Butterfields 3-24-03 (A)

Brooch, high karat gold, Victorian bird motif of naturalistic form, set throughout with old mine-cut diamonds and antique cushion-cut emeralds, sapphires, and rubies, embellished with multi-colored polychrome enamel; estimated total diamond weight: 3 cts. (loss to enamel, stones).

Price: $3,819

Photo courtesy Skinner 12/9/03 (A)

Brooch, micro mosaic butterfly composed of multicolored tesserae, gilt frame and bail with wirework and bead accents.

Price: $1,293

Photo courtesy Skinner 12/9/03 (A)

Brooch, Egyptian Revival, 14k gold and enamel, centering a carved rose quartz scarab with enameled wings, framed by asps, with enameled lotus flower drop, European hallmarks.

Price: $999

Messada Antiques (D)

Brooch, circa 1870s, French stone cameo, octagonal with an oval in the center, pierced work.

Price: $7,140, £4,250

Jewelry Box Antiques (D)

Brooch, circa 1870s, 14k yellow gold with taille d' épergne enamel, approximately 1-1/14" diameter.
Price: $395

John Joseph (D)

Brooch, circa 1875, 15k gold, mythological scene, approximately 2-1/2" x 3" long.
Price: $2,880, £1,600

John Joseph (D)

Brooch, circa 1870s, Renaissance Revival, sapphire and pearls with short and long stem for wearing as a brooch or stickpin, 3" x 1-1/2".
Price: $12,600, £7,000

Charlotte Sayer (D)

Brooch, circa 1880s, ivory, sheaves of wheat motif, 7 cm x 4-1/2 cm.
Price: $630, £350

John Joseph (D)

Backside of brooch.

Brooch, circa 1870s, 15k gold, cabochon garnet, glazed compartment for hair, 2" x 2-3/4" long, including detachable drop.

Price: $1,980, £1,100

Back view of brooch.

Brooch, circa 1870s, Renaissance Revival style, large pinkish topaz, white and green enamel, screw back removable pin stem.

Michael Shers (D)

Price: $6,000

Messada Antiques (D)

Designs by Irene (D)

Brooch, circa 1880s, 15k gold, serpent motif with cut garnet, ruby eyes, beautifully engraved, 1-1/4".

Price: $650

Brooch, circa 1880s, Etruscan work, revival-inspired piece.

Price: $1,791, £995

Messada Antiques (D)

Jane Fletcher (D)

Brooch, circa 1880s, tortoiseshell, cherub motif.

Price: $450

Brooch, circa 1880s, micro mosaic, red glass background, well done, glazed compartment in back, perfect condition.

Price: $2,475, £1,375

Sharen Duncan-August (D)

Brooch, circa 1880s, Venetian mosaic pansy motif set in goldstone.

Price: $400

Brooch, circa 1880s, gold set with goldstone, Venetian mosaic.

Price: $480

Sharen Duncan-August (D)

Brooch, circa 1880s, micro mosaic of a seated lady.

Price: $1,700

Jane Fletcher (D)

Brooch, circa 1880s, green enamel background with descending dove set with half pearls, rubies, and emeralds, 3-3/4" x 3".

Price: $2,600

Old World Jewelry (D)

Brooch, circa 1880, 18k pietre dure with pansy motif.

Price: $1,150

Jane Fletcher (D)

Code by photograph credit line:

(A) Auction House—Auction Price

(C) Collector—Collector Asking Price

(D) Dealer—Dealer Asking Price

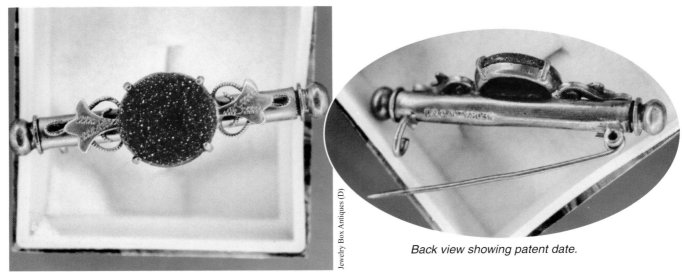

Jewelry Box Antiques (D)

Back view showing patent date.

Brooch, circa 1880s, rolled gold set with goldstone, end opens to reveal container holding needles and surrounded with thread.

Price: $400

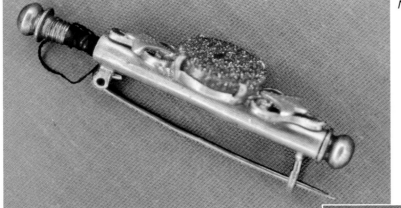

Needle case pulled out from side.

Thread wrapped around needle holder.

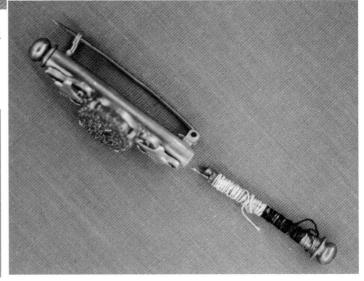

Code by photograph credit line:

(A) Auction House—Auction Price

(C) Collector—Collector Asking Price

(D) Dealer—Dealer Asking Price

Brooch, circa 1880, 18k pietre dure, yellow flowers.
Price: $1,150

Jane Fletcher (D)

Photo courtesy Skinner 6/17/03 (A)

Brooch, silver topped 14k gold mount, enamel and diamond butterfly with red, yellow, blue, and black basse taille enamel wings and old mine-cut diamond body, ruby eyes, rose-cut diamond accents, Austro-Hungarian hallmarks.

Price: $6,463

John Joseph (D)

Brooch, circa 1860-'80s, 15k gold set with oval cabochon garnet, glazed compartment in back, 1-1/2" x 1-1/8".
Price: $1,251, £695

Sue Brown (D)

Brooch, circa 1880s, winged carved cornelian scarab.
Price: $710, £395

Sue Brown (D)

Brooch, circa 1880s, pietre dure with bird motif.
Price: $1,512, £840

Sue Brown (D)

Brooch, circa 1880s, pietre dure with bird motif.
Price: $1,512, £840

Brooch, circa 1880s, gold over brass, made of watch cock covers set with garnets, pearls, and turquoise.

Price: $475

Brooch, circa 1880s, gold over brass, star burst with garnets, 1-3/8" diameter.

Price: $495

Back view of brooch.

Brooch, circa 1880s, gold over brass, made from three watch cock covers.

Price: $325

Brooch, circa 1880s, amethyst and pearls set in a pansy motif.

Price: $1,050

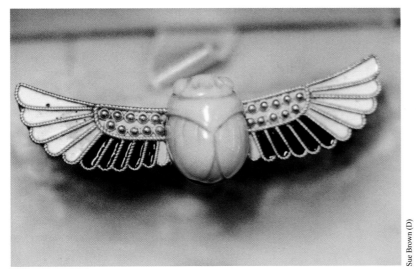

Brooch, circa 1880s, Egyptian revival, scarab, pink angel skin coral with enamel wings.
Price: $1,433.95, £850

Sue Brown (D)

Old World Jewelry (D)

Brooch, circa 1880s, painting on porcelain, Vagabond Boy, 2-1/2" x 2".
Price: $350

Jeanenne Bell (C)

Brooch, circa 1880, 18k yellow gold set with cornelian cameo with cherub surrounded by seed pearls, 1-1/2" x 1-1/4".
Price: $1,250

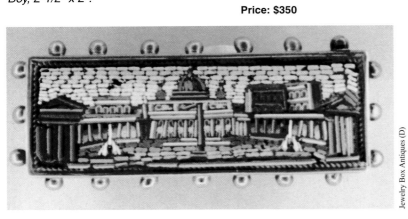

Jewelry Box Antiques (D)

Brooch, gold micro mosaic, 1-1/2" x-1/2".
Price: $750

Brooch, circa 1880, 14k gold with wire work design, 2-1/2" x-3/4".

Price: $575

Jewelry Box Antiques (D)

Brooch, circa 1880, yellow gold-filled, shell cameo, 1-3/4" x 1-1/2".

Price: $225

Jewelry Box Antiques (D)

Code by photograph credit line:

(A) Auction House—Auction Price

(C) Collector—Collector Asking Price

(D) Dealer—Dealer Asking Price

Brooch, circa 1880, multi gold top brass back.

Price: $175

Jewelry Box Antiques (D)

Cufflinks

Brookside Antiques (D)

Collar buttons and cufflinks, circa 1860-'70s.

Price, Onyx flowers: $225
Price, Banded agate: $425
Price, Oak leaf: $275

Earrings

Launder Antiques (D)

Earrings, circa 1860s, pique, ball top with dangle bottom with beautiful floral motif.
Price: $1,035, £575

Launder Antiques (D)

Earrings, circa 1860, jet dangle, carved flowers.
Price: $557, £310

Messada Antiques (D)

Closer view of bird design.

Earrings, circa 1860s, pique design of birds and flowers, overall length 2".
Price: $1,150, £600

Messada Antiques (D)

Earrings, circa 1860-'70s, Swiss enamel painting on porcelain, girls in native costume, bottom dangles removable for day wear.
Price: $1,750 £925

Sharen Duncan-August (D)

Earrings, circa 1860s, wheat sheaves motif.

Price: $350

Jane Fletcher (D)

Earrings, circa 1860s, 15k gold Etruscan work, all original.
Price: $1,100

Sharen Duncan-August (D)

Earrings, circa 1860s, cut steel set with painting on porcelain.

Price: $600

Veritas (D)

Earrings, circa 1860s, gold, table worked hair.

Price: $550

Sue Brown (D)

Earrings, circa 1860s, pique, Grecian urn design.
Price: $2,700, £1,500

Earrings, circa 1870s, cut steel.

Price: $550, £305

Launder Antiques (D)

Veritas (D)

Earrings, circa 1870s, pietre dure.

Price: $1,750

Photo courtesy Bonhams and Butterfields 3-24-03 (A)

Earrings,14k gold frame, each round, bombé form earring set with mine-, old mine-, and table-cut diamonds, the high karat gold openwork mount set atop blue enamel, completed by a screw back, estimated total diamond weight for the pair: 1.75 cts.

Price: $2,350

Jane Fletcher (D)

Earrings, circa 1880, 18k, carved coral, in original box.

Price: $1,100

Earrings, circa 1880, pietre dure, 1-1/2" x 3/4".

Messada Antiques (D)

Price: $1,350, £750

Photo courtesy Bonhams and Butterfields 3-24-03 (A)

Earrings, 19th century, 18k gold and silver, pearls and diamonds, each pendant earring topped by a button-shaped pearl measuring approximately 10.50 mm x 8.50 mm x 9 mm and 10 mm x 10 mm x 5.50 mm, suspending a small gold floret set with old mine- and rose-cut diamonds, terminating with a drop-shaped natural pearl measuring 19.90 mm x 12.35 mm x 9.90 mm and 18 mm x 11.60 mm x 9.30 mm, the silver bell caps set with white sapphires. Accompanied by G.I.A. Gem Trade Laboratory report #12395187, dated Dec. 20, 2002, stating the drop-shaped pearls as: Natural Pearls (button pearls not tested for origin).

Price: $12,925

Launder Antiques (D)

Earrings, circa 1880s, 15k set with diamonds with dark green and white enamel.

Price: $1,856, £1,100

Jeanenne Bell (C)

Earrings, circa 1880s, brass, made of cock covers from 18th century watches, new ear wires.

Price: $295

Lockets

Messada Antiques (D)

Locket, circa 1860s, 18k gold, double-sided glazed compartments, 2-1/4" long x 1-1/4" wide.
Price: $1,665, £925

Messada Antiques (D)

Locket, 18k gold, double-sided glazed compartments, wire work.
Price: $1,512, £840

Brookside Antiques (D)

Locket, circa 1870-'80s, 10k gold with rose-cut diamond, 1" x 1-1/2".
Price: $575

Nunsuch Antiques (D)

Locket and chain, circa 1870s, 14k gold, 1ct. oval diamond, two glazed compartments, locket 2-1/2" x 1-3/4", chain 17" long.
Price: $2,000

Back view of locket.

Locket, circa 1870-'80s, sterling silver with engraved links, locket is embellished with pink-gold and green-gold birds, locket 1-3/8" x 2-3/8", chain approximately 18" long.

Jewelry Box Antiques (D)

Price: $950

Messada Antiques (D)

Code by photograph credit line:

(A) Auction House—Auction Price

(C) Collector—Collector Asking Price

(D) Dealer—Dealer Asking Price

Locket, circa 1880, 18k gold, star setting with diamond, two glazed compartments, 2" long x 1" wide.

Price: $1,296, £720

Messada Antiques (D)

Back view of locket showing compartment for hair.

Locket, circa 1880s, pietre dure, slate with roses and flowers, compartment for hair in back.
Price: $1,026, £570

Code by photograph credit line:

(A) Auction House—Auction Price

(C) Collector—Collector Asking Price

(D) Dealer—Dealer Asking Price

Locket, 18k gold, polychrome enamel, openwork trellis of light blue, white, and red blossoms.
Price: $999

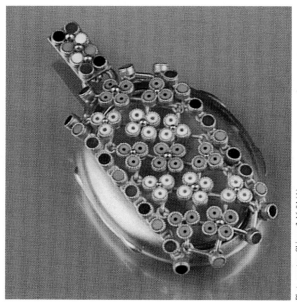

Photo courtesy Skinner 3-16-04 (A)

Necklaces

Launder Antiques (D)

Necklace, circa 1860s, pique interspersed with gold balls, 18"-19" long.

Price: $3,374, £2,000

Veritas (D)

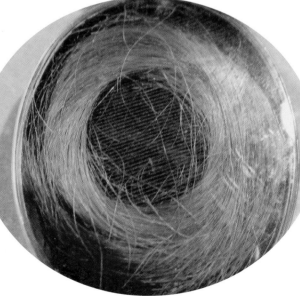

Back view showing lock of hair.

Necklace, circa 1860s, painted photograph of young girl with hair in compartment in back, suspended from a hair work chain.

Price: $680

Necklace, antique, set throughout with faceted garnets in a graduating floret design, gilt-metal mount, 1g., 14-1/2" long (missing one stone).

Price: $1,762

Photo courtesy Skinner, Boston 12-9-03 (A)

Code by photograph credit line:

(A) Auction House—Auction Price

(C) Collector—Collector Asking Price

(D) Dealer—Dealer Asking Price

Nunsuch Antiques (D)

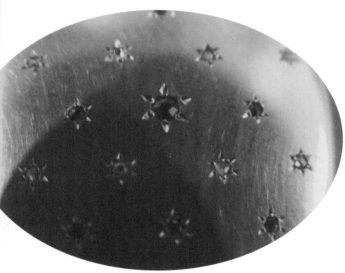

Closer view of stone setting.

Necklace, circa 1860s, gold set with sapphires, original book chain, locket, 2-1/4" x 1-1/2" wide.

Price: $1,890, £1,050

Charlotte Sayer (D)

Necklace, circa 1860s, jet with cherub painted on porcelain, 4 cm x 4-1/2 cm long, chain 50 cm long.

Price: $990, £550

Jewelry Box Antiques (D)

Necklace, circa 1860-'80s, yellow gold-filled book chain design, chain 18" long, locket 1-1/4" x 7/8".

Price: $650

Courtville Antiques (D)

Necklace, circa 1860s, bog oak, castle and abbey scenes.

Price: $495

Necklace, circa 1870s, multi-gold birds, stone cameo with pearls, original chain, glazed compartment in back, 2-1/4" x 1-1/4", chain 17" long.

Price: $4,800

Brookside Antiques (D)

Code by photograph credit line:

(A) Auction House—Auction Price

(C) Collector—Collector Asking Price

(D) Dealer—Dealer Asking Price

Veritas (D)

Close-up of central plaque.

Necklace, circa 1870s, Italian, coral, leaves and bird center plaque.

Price: $1,050

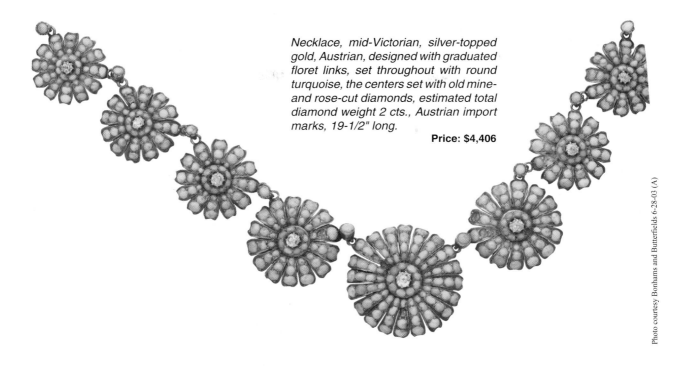

Necklace, mid-Victorian, silver-topped gold, Austrian, designed with graduated floret links, set throughout with round turquoise, the centers set with old mine- and rose-cut diamonds, estimated total diamond weight 2 cts., Austrian import marks, 19-1/2" long.

Price: $4,406

Photo courtesy Bonhams and Butterfields 6-28-03 (A)

Close-up of snake head.

Necklace, circa 1870s, snake with heart drop, mine-cut diamonds, 16" long.

Price: $8,100, £4,500

John Joseph (D)

Pendant with chain, Russian aquamarine, diamond, gold, and silver, pendant featuring a pear-shaped aquamarine weighing approximately 20 cts., framed in 14k yellow gold, surmounted by a bow motif silver-topped gold bail, set with mine- and rose-cut diamonds; suspended from a fine link silver chain, partial hallmarks, possibly "AM" for work master Anders Mickelson, for Faberge.

Price: $3,231

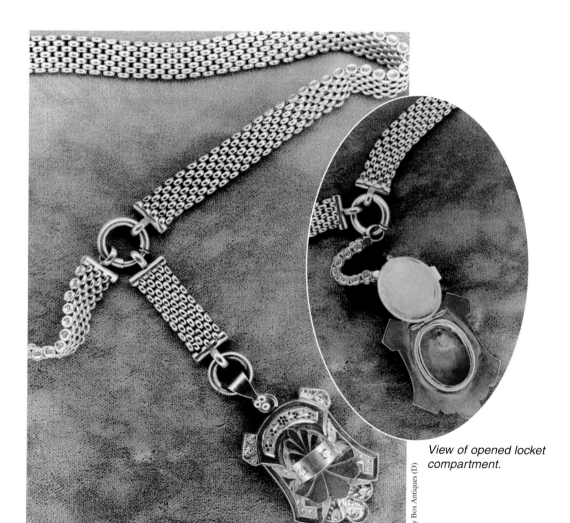

Photo courtesy Bonhams and Butterfields 6-24-03 (A)

Jewelry Box Antiques (D)

View of opened locket compartment.

Necklace, circa 1870s, rolled gold mesh chain with pendant locket.

Price: $850

Silver-topped gold necklace, French Victorian diamond, central ornament of stylized bow form, completed by tapering oval links, further completed by bar links, set throughout with mine-, rose-, old single, and antique cushion-cut diamonds, estimated total diamond weight 6.50 cts., 16 5/8" long, French marks.

Price: $9,200

Necklace, circa 1880s, opal and diamond.

Price: $20,700, £12,500

Messada Antiques (D)

Photo courtesy Bonhams and Butterfields 3-24-03 (A)

Chain, circa 1880, gold, French, Grecian key design, 20" long.

Price: $2,600

Veritas (D)

Necklace, circa 1880-'90s, 14k festoon, coral cameos.

Price: $1,750

Stone Home Antiques (D)

Necklace, circa 1880-'90s, 14k gold set with aquamarine and seed pearls.

Price: $1,800

Stone Home Antiques (D)

Necklace, circa 1860-'80s, yellow gold-filled with turquoise and pearls, 24" long.

Price: $525

Jewelry Box Antiques (D)

Code by photograph credit line:

(A) Auction House—Auction Price

(C) Collector—Collector Asking Price

(D) Dealer—Dealer Asking Price

Pendant necklace, Renaissance Revival, 18k gold, enamel and gem-set pendant with Limoges enamel depiction of Hesperus, god of the evening star, in his chariot, frame and bail with tendrils in pink, white, and black enamel with square-cut diamond and sapphire highlights, suspended by a conforming delicate fancy link chain, 26.3 dwt, 1g., 19" long.

Price: $4,583

Photo courtesy Skinner 12/9/03 (A)

Jewelry Box Antiques (D)

Necklace, circa 1880s, yellow gold-filled mesh with stone cameo.

Price: $675

Jeanenne Bell (C)

Necklace, circa 1880s, rolled gold book chain with original locket with painting on porcelain.
Price: $995

Necklace, circa 1880s, gold over brass, made of watch cock covers from 18th century watches.

Price: $700

Jeanenne Bell (C)

Necklace, circa 1880-'90s, gold over brass, made of watch cock covers.

Price: $675

Jeanenne Bell (C)

Necklace, circa late 1880s, gold over brass, made of watch cock covers.

Price: $700

Jeanenne Bell (C)

Necklace, circa 1880s, book chain with crescent drop set with imitation pearls and doublets.

Price: $400

Jewelry Box Antiques (D)

Renada Ramsey (D)

Necklace, circa 1880s, yellow gold-filled book chain, mine-cut brilliant in center, Etruscan work, locket 2" long x 1-1/8" wide, chain 18" long.

Price: $525

Code by photograph credit line:

(A) Auction House—Auction Price

(C) Collector—Collector Asking Price

(D) Dealer—Dealer Asking Price

Pendants

Jewelry Box Antiques (D)

Pendant, circa 1860s, gutta-percha, 3-1/2" x 1 7/8".
Price: $300

Launders Antiques (D)

Pendant, circa 1860s, Whitby jet, ball of jet on the inside.

Price: $590, £350

Pendant/brooch, circa 1850-'60s, enameled bleeding heart motif, centered with diamond forget-me-not.
Price: $3,600, £2,150

Messada Antiques (D)

Jewelry Box Antiques (D)

Pendant, circa 1860s, jet with painting on porcelain of the Vagabond Boy, 2-1/4" x 1-1/2".

Price: $450

Messada Antiques (D)

Pendant, circa 1865, pique heart motif, 1-1/4" x 1".

Price: $1,125, £625

Sue Brown (D)

Pendant, circa 1860s, heavy gold scarab with a locket back.

Price: $4,217, £2,500

Photo courtesy Skinner, Boston 6/17/03 (A)

Pendant/brooch, silver topped 14k gold mount set with diamond and sapphire, centered with a bezel-set oval sapphire measuring approximately 10.10 mm x 7.85 mm x 5.05 mm, surrounded by fifty-eight old mine-cut, old European, and single-cut diamonds, approximate total weight 5.56 cts.

Price: $8,225

Pendant, circa 1860s, carved ivory locket.
Price: $650

Different view of pendant.

Pendant, cross gutta-percha, 2-3/4" x 1-3/4".
Price: $250

Pendant, circa 1860-'70s, Whitby jet, shown with jet brooch.

Price, Brooch: $371, £220
Price, Pendant: $540, £320

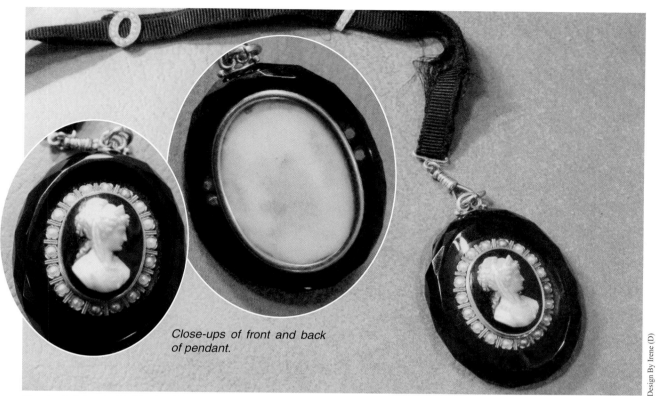

Close-ups of front and back of pendant.

Design By Irene (D)

Pendant, jet set with black with white stone cameo, on original grosgrain ribbon that has two slides set with half seed pearls, 2" x 1-1/2".

Price: $1,350

Photo courtesy Sotheby's of London 12-03-03 (A)

Pendant, circa 1870, gold and rock crystal reverse intaglio, oval, depicting a goldfinch perched on a branch, within a border of corded wire and beaded decoration, glazed compartment in back.

Price: $1,728

Pendant, amethyst intaglio and chain embellishes with emeralds and rubies, 2-1/2" x 1-3/4".
Price: $18,900, £10,500

Messada Antiques (D)

Old World Jewelry (D)

Reverse side showing two compartments for hair and engraved inscription.

Pendant, circa 1870s, gold cross, mine- and rose-cut diamonds and pearls, engraved "Lucy Countess of Paris Born Sept. 23, 1793 Died Sept. 16, 1875," two compartments for hair.
Price: $2,200

Messada Antiques (D)

Pendant, circa 1870s, blue enamel and pearls, star burst design, 1-1/4" x 2".
Price: $1,710, £950

Messada Antiques (D)

Pendant, circa 1860-'70s, star burst design, set with half pearls, dark royal blue and white enamel, 2" long.
Price: $1,224, £680

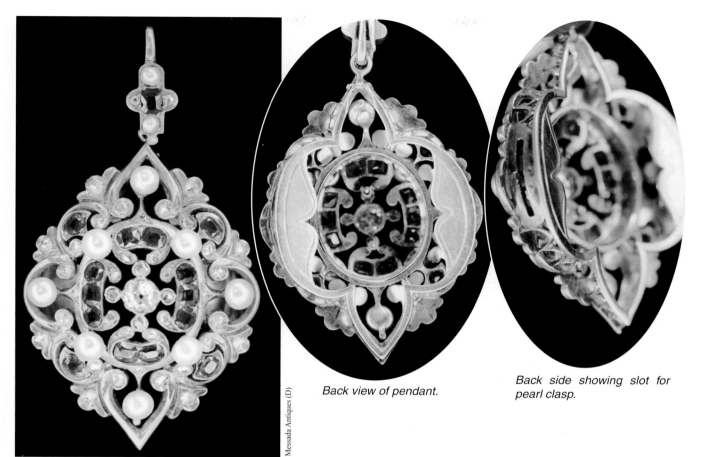

Messada Antiques (D)

Back view of pendant.

Back side showing slot for pearl clasp.

Pendant, circa 1870s, Burma rubies, diamonds, and pearls, has brooch fittings and clasp fittings at side to wear on a mesh chain or pearls as central plaque.

Price: $9,995, £5,950

Photo courtesy Sotheby's of London 12-16-03 (A)

Pendant, circa 1878, the oval mourning locket applied with a black enamel ground and a cushion-shaped and rose-cut diamond monogram "MC" and Spanish crown, suspended from a similarly set diamond pendant loop, the reverse decorated with a gold cross and inscription "22de Agosto 1878," opening to reveal a glazed hair compartment. The diamond-set initials "MC" below the Spanish crown are those of Maria Cristina, Queen Regent of Spain from Sept. 29, 1833, to Sept. 17, 1840. Born Princess Maria Cristina of the Two-Sicilies, 1802, and died Aug. 22, 1878, she married as his fourth wife King Fernando VII of Spain (1784-1844) and secondly (and morganatically) Fernando Munoz y Sanchez, Duke of Riansares, Grandee of Spain. Pendant is the property of a member of a German royal family.

Price: $4,752, £2,640

Jeanenne Bell (D)

Pendant/brooch, circa 1870-'80s, 15k gold, sardonyx cameo with grandulation, 1-1/8" x 1 7/8".
Price: $1,400

Charlotte Sayer (D)

Pendant, circa 1870-'80s, ivory cross, 6 cm x 3-3/4 cm.
Price: $505, £280

Jewelry Box Antiques (D)

Pendant, circa 1880s, gold over brass Venetian mosaic cross, 1-3/4" x 2".
Price: $250

Sue Brown (D)

Pendant, circa 1880s, pietre dure Maltese cross.
Price: $650, £330

Pendant, circa 1880s, peridot with pearls, 2" x 1".
Price: $1,665 (pendant only), £925

Messada Antiques (D)

*Compartment in
the back for hair.*

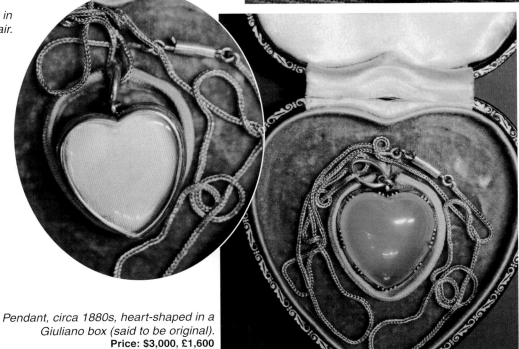

*Pendant, circa 1880s, heart-shaped in a
Giuliano box (said to be original).*
Price: $3,000, £1,600

Sue Brown (D)

Pendant, circa 1880s, gold mounting, goldstone, micro mosaic, 1-1/2" x 1-3/4".

Price: $2,070, £1,150

Messada Antiques (D)

Michael Sher (D)

Pendant, circa 1880, reverse intaglio in crystal carved from back and hand painted, button made into a pendant (green back heron).

Price: $1,500

Bernard Cohen (D)

Pendant, circa 1880-'90s, sterling silver locket, English hallmark, 1-3/4" x 1-1/2".

Price: $200

Code by photograph credit line:

(A) Auction House—Auction Price

(C) Collector—Collector Asking Price

(D) Dealer—Dealer Asking Price

Code by photograph credit line:

(A) Auction House—Auction Price

(C) Collector—Collector Asking Price

(D) Dealer—Dealer Asking Price

Veritas (D)

Pendant, circa 1880s, gold cross, hair work.
Price: $180

Closer view of coral pendant.

Veritas (D)

Pendant, circa 1880, coral cameo with original chain.
Price: $950

Photo courtesy Sotheby's of London 12-16-03 (A)

Pendant/brooch, last quarter of the 19th century, oval, hardstone cameo depicting a maiden facing right, within a border decorated with half pearls, later fittings.

Price: $1,296, £720

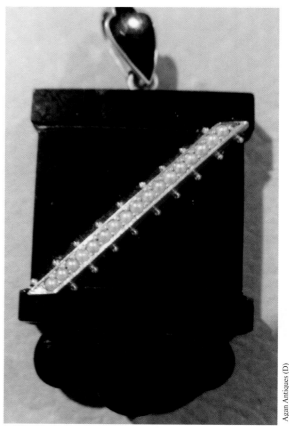

Agan Antiques (D)

Pendant, circa 1880s, onyx and gold, black enamel bale, reverse has glazed compartment for hair, 2 5/8" x 1-1/4".

Price: $350

Photo courtesy Skinner 12/9/03 (A)

Pendant, Victorian 18k gold, Edwin Streeter, enamel, bezel-set with a carbuncle, white enamel, wire, and beadwork accents, signed EMS, successors to Hancock & Co., original fitted box.

Price: $2,232.50

Launder Antiques (D)

Pendant, circa 1880s, 15k gold locket.

Price: $890, £495

Pins

Stickpin, circa 1880s, carved carnelian scarab with enamel wings.
Price: $666, £395

Sue Brown (D)

Stickpin, gold head embellished with enamel, diamond, and pearl.
Price: $900

Jewelry Box Antiques (D)

Bar pin, circa 1880-'90s, rubies and diamonds, 2" long x 1/2" wide.
Price: $891, £495

Messada Antiques (D)

Pin, circa 1880s, silver-topped 14k gold mount, designed as a coiled rose-cut diamond serpent with ruby eyes, Austro-Hungarian hallmark.
Price: $1,058

Photo courtesy Skinner 6-17-03 (A)

Stickpin, circa 1880s, gold set with stone cameo with three faces, 1/2" diameter.
Price: $900

Michael Sheer (D)

Bar pin, 14k gold, sugarloaf garnet surrounded by rose-cut diamonds set throughout with faceted garnets, French hallmarks (missing one stone).
Price: $1,068

Photo courtesy Skinner 3-16-04 (A)

Rings

Charlotte Sayer (D)

Ring, circa 1860s, 18k gold, hands separate to reveal a heart inside.

Price: $1,710, £950

Messada Antiques (D)

Ring, 1866 hallmark, 18k gold set with crystalite.

Price: $630, £350

Close-up detail showing three separate rings.

Code by photograph credit line:

(A) Auction House—Auction Price

(C) Collector—Collector Asking Price

(D) Dealer—Dealer Asking Price

Ring, circa 1860-'70s, 14k yellow gold centered with oval amethyst with incised carving of a flower inset with gold and rose-cut diamond, mounting embellished with taille d' épergne enamel.

Price: $1,500

Jeanenne Bell (C)

Jeanenne Bell (C)

Ring, circa 1860s, 18k yellow gold, full figure stone cameo.

Price: $995

Jewelry Box Antiques (D)

Ring, circa 1850-'60s, 14k yellow gold with onyx stone cameo.

Price: $675

Jewelry Box Antiques (D)

Ring, circa 1860-'70s, 10k gold cigar band style set with natural ruby.

Price: $400

Jewelry Box Antiques (D)

Ring, circa 1860-'70s, 10k gold set with amethyst, small scale for child or small lady.

Price: $425

Jewelry Box Antiques (D)

Ring, circa 1860-'70s, 10k gold set with garnet and glass doublet and two seed pearls, small scale for child or small lady.

Price: $375

Ring, circa 1860-'70s, gold, painting on porcelain of Vagabond Boy motif.

Price: $375

Ring, circa 1860-'70s, gold set with cabochon garnet.

Price: $550

Ring, circa 1870s, turquoise and pearl with glazed compartment underneath center.

Price: $650

Back view showing compartment for hair.

Ring, hallmark 1883, 18k gold set with pearls and rubies.

Price: $630, £350

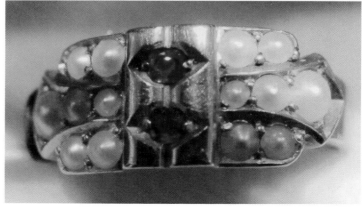

Sets

Messada Antiques (D)

Earrings and brooch, circa 1860-'70s, 18k
earrings 3-1/4" x-3/4", brooch 1-1/2" x 3-1/2",
Tuscan style, brooch can also be worn as a
pendant.

Price: $17,730, £9,850

Photo courtesy Bonhams and Butterfields 6-24-03 (A)

Photo courtesy Sotheby's of London (A)

Necklace and brooch, silver set with lava cameo, necklace designed
as a graduated row of lava cameos depicting various female profiles
facing left and right, length approximately 430 mm; the brooch en
suite, cameo cracked.

Price: $2,600/$3,400, £1,800

Brooch and earrings, 18k gold set with an oval
micro mosaic depicting an Italian architectural
scene, embellished with wire work, suspending
three drop pendants; together with a pair of
earrings of similar design, each mosaic depicting
an historic Italian ruin.

Price: $1,200/$1,800

Photo courtesy Skinner, Boston 9/23/03 (A)

Brooch and earrings, 14k gold set with amethyst, a knot with sprays of amethyst berries, applied wire twist decoration, glass compartment verso, earrings en suite.

Price: $1,410

Jewelry Box Antiques (D)

Brooch and earrings, jet with painted porcelain plaques featuring Vagabond Boy, 2-3/4" x 1 7/8", earrings 2" x 3/4".

Price: $1,800

Jeanenne Bell (C)

Brooch and earrings, circa 1870s, gold top with gold over brass backs and taille d' épergne enameling, centered with black/white stone cameos.

Price: $1,100

Code by photograph credit line:

(A) Auction House—Auction Price

(C) Collector—Collector Asking Price

(D) Dealer—Dealer Asking Price

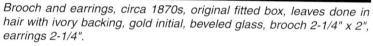

Bernard Cohen (D)

Matching earrings.

Brooch and earrings, circa 1870s, original fitted box, leaves done in hair with ivory backing, gold initial, beveled glass, brooch 2-1/4" x 2", earrings 2-1/4".

Price: $4,000

Beverly Tarren (D)

Brooch and earrings, circa 1870s, lava cameos set in silver, earrings elongated (day and night), bottom removes for day wear, brooch 1-1/2" x 1-3/4", earrings 2" x 1/2" across.

Price: $850

Photo courtesy Sotheby's of London 12-16-03 (A)

Bracelet, brooch, and a pair of pendant earrings, mid-19th century, demi-parure, each set with lava cameo of putti in high relief within plain yellow gold frames, bracelet length 210 mm approximately, earrings have hoop fittings, leather case. The Goldsmith and Silversmiths Company Ltd., Regent Street, London.

Price: $4,752, £2,640

Necklace and pendant, circa 1870-'80s, onyx necklace measuring 18" with drop and cross set with seed pearls, total length 23".

Price: $895

Michelle Davidson (C)

Code by photograph credit line:

(A) Auction House—Auction Price

(C) Collector—Collector Asking Price

(D) Dealer—Dealer Asking Price

Old World Antiques (D)

Cameo set, original fitted box, brooch 4" x 3-1/2", three different layers of stone, Archeological Revival influence.

Price: $9,600

Joan Stern (D)

Brooch and earring set, circa 1870s, 14k gold, black taille d' épergne enamel, brooch 1-3/4" wide x 2-1/4" long, earrings 1/4" wide x 2" long.
Price: $1,875

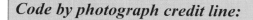

Code by photograph credit line:

(A) Auction House—Auction Price

(C) Collector—Collector Asking Price

(D) Dealer—Dealer Asking Price

Design By Irene (D)

Close-up showing detail.

Brooch and earrings set, 14k, diamond in center with fringe, brooch 1-7/8" wide x 2-1/2" long, earrings 1-3/4" wide x 2".
Price: $2,200

Old World Jewelry (D)

Brooch and earrings set, Etruscan Revival, cabochon garnet in center with square garnets on sides, brooch 2-1/2" x 1-1/2", earrings 3-3/4" x 1/2".

Price: $1,850

Designs by Irene (D)

Brooch and earrings set, circa 1870s, 18k gold and pearls, original box, brooch 3-1/4" x 1-1/2", earrings 2-1/4" x 3/8".

Price: $2,250

Designs by Irene (D)

Brooch and earrings set, circa 1870s, natural pearls and granulation.

Price: $1,850

Renata Ransby (D)

Brooch and earrings set, circa 1870-'80s, coral cameos, brooch, 1-3/4" x 1-1/4", earrings 1-1/4" x 3/4".

Price: $1,400

Brooch and earrings set, circa 1880s, bog oak, round disk top, 1-1/4" diameter with drop on bottom, 3/4" x 1/2", earrings overall 7/8" x 3/8".

Price: $350

A Lady's Gallery (D)

Messada Antiques (D)

Brooch and earrings set, circa 1888, 15k engraved, glazed compartment on back, 1-1/2" diameter.

Price: $2,520, £1,335

Photo courtesy Skinner, Boston 6/17/03 (A)

Brooch and ear pendants, Victorian 14k bi-color gold and coral demi-parure, the brooch designed as scroll-handed scissors snipping bunches of angelskin coral grapes from a leafy vine, ear pendants en suite.

Price: $1,880

Code by photograph credit line:

(A) Auction House—Auction Price

(C) Collector—Collector Asking Price

(D) Dealer—Dealer Asking Price

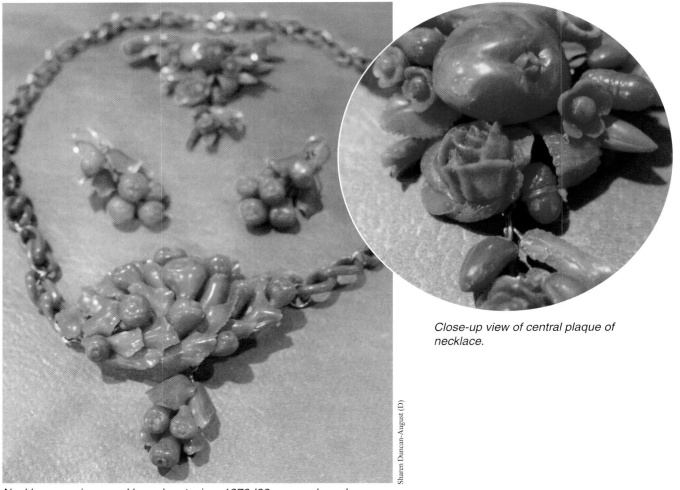

Sharen Duncan-August (D)

Close-up view of central plaque of necklace.

Necklace, earrings, and brooch set, circa 1870-'80s, carved coral.
Price: $2,000

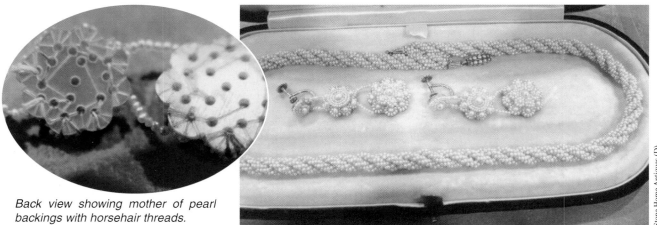

Back view showing mother of pearl backings with horsehair threads.

Stone Home Antiques (D)

Necklace and earrings set, circa 1880s, seed pearls, original box, earring screws not original.

Price: $3,500

Fringe necklace, Archaeological Revival, 18k gold and coral demi-parure, composed of twenty-five coral cameos of bacchante maidens suspended from tubular links interspersed with disc-shaped gold beads, bead and wirework accents, completed by an "S" clasp mounted with a cameo, ear pendants en suite, made by Melillo, with original fitted box. Provenance: This demi-parure has descended in one family since its purchase.

Price: $42,300

Watches

Pocket watch, circa 1880, 18k yellow gold, bezel and back set with seed pearls, circular, open face, bezel and back set with red translucent enamel, with enamel scene on back; Bristol Goldsmiths Alliance Company, English gold and enamel case; dial: white enamel, black Roman numerals, blued steel "spade" hands; movement: gilt, jeweled, lever escapement, cut bi-metallic screwed balance wheel, Breguet balance spring. Signed Langford on movement. Diameter: 31 mm. Note: Also signed Bristol Goldsmiths Alliance Company.

Price: $1,300

Photo courtesy Bonhams & Butterfield 12/16/03 (A)

Jewelry Box Antiques (D)

Watch pin, circa 1880s, gold top with brass back.

Price: $125

Jewelry Box Antiques (D)

Watch chain, circa 1880s, yellow gold-filled, black stone fob.

Price: $110

Jewelry Box Antiques (D)

Fob-locket, circa 1880s, 14k gold with cornelian on one lid and onyx on the other.

Price: $350

Miscellaneous

Watch fob and chain, 18k gold, designed as a squirrel grasping a nut, suspended from three open chased and engraved links with varied C-scroll and ruffle, foliate, and floral motifs, 55.9 dwt. Lg. 6-1/2", signed Tiffany & Co., original box.

Price: $6,463

Photo courtesy Skinner 9/23/03 (A)

SECTION IV

1890-1901 TIMELINE

1890—Charles Danna Gibson's "Gibson Girl" makes her debut.
Torch is developed that is hot enough to make working platinum easier.
Platinum becomes the most popular metal.

1891— The bruting machine is invented, which makes the girdle of a stone round. First truly round diamonds are created.

1893—Columbian Exposition held in Chicago.

1893-'97—Grover Cleveland is president of the United States.

1897-'01—William McKinley is president of the United States.

1897—Queen Victoria's Diamond Jubilee.

1898—Alaskan gold rush.

1898—America declares war on Spain.

1899-1902—Boer War in South Africa.

1900—Queen Victoria's son, Alfred, dies.

1901—Queen Victoria dies on Tuesday, Jan. 22.

1901—First transatlantic signal sent by wireless telegraph.

1890 - 1901

The 1890s in the United Stated and Great Britain were filled with exciting new developments. The "gay nineties" referred to the mood of many in society. Both countries were taking on airs of worldliness, but still had some of the innocence of youth. It seemed that everyone wanted to shake off the heavy, sometimes stifling traditions of the past along with the heavy and cumbersome styles of Victorian clothes.

By 1890 more women were involved in the world of business. By 1910 there were 386,765 women employed in offices, an increase of 385,835 since 1870. Women were also playing the stock market. The first brokerage firm owned by a woman opened on Wall Street in 1869 and was an immediate success. Women could become rich by investing in the market, but they still could not vote.

Workers had more leisure time than they had ever experienced on the farm. Entertainment was a booming business during these years. In 1893 Thomas Edison invented the kintoscope, which required a nickel for operation. It didn't take long for these "nickelodeons" to become a popular form of entertainment. Theater was also thriving. Comic acts and all forms of vaudeville acts stayed busy traveling from city to city. The new middle class of people had money, many for the first time, and they wanted to be entertained.

The bicycle had been popular since the 1860s, but women's fashions had kept it from being enjoyed by the fairer sex. With the softening of their clothing and their liberation from cumbersome skirts and bustles, women could now begin to ride comfortably, and the bicycle became the plaything of the 1890s. Men, women, and children of all ages spent every possible minute riding the many varieties available. The demand was so great that companies in totally unrelated businesses began to manufacture bicycles. By 1896 Chester Frost & Company, wholesale jewelry manufacturers, included bicycles in its

catalog. It proudly advertised, "The bicycle is no longer simply a luxury or a toy for children and idle men but an article of everyday necessity for thousands." The biggest seller weighed 25 pounds and sold for $100. Other bicycles were priced from $94 to $120.

Godey's Lady's Book estimated in 1896 that there were 10 million bicycles in the world, and cyclists traveled more than 100 million miles. In Paris there was a riding school on the Champs Elysees. For $4, one could attend until "thoroughly proficient." According to *Godey's,* there was even a bicycle ambulance: "The bicycle ambulance is a humanitarian invention for removing sick people; it runs more easily and makes less noise than the regulation vehicle. It has met with instantaneous success in Chicago."

The Delineator Magazine *from March 1896.*

For those who couldn't afford a bicycle, here was a chance to earn one. The advertisement ran in the May 1899 issue of Ladies Home Journal.

In England there was also a bicycle craze. As the Rev. John Rusk stated in his book, *The Beautiful Life and Illustrious Reign of Queen Victoria*:

The Queen gave her countenance to ladies riding the tricycle at a very early stage of the introduction of that machine. It was while taking her favorite drive along the Newport Road in the Isle of Wight that she for the first time saw a lady riding a tricycle, and she was so much pleased that she ordered two machines to be sent to Osborne for some of her ladies to learn to ride upon. When the more expeditious bicycle came into use, Her Majesty looked askance for a time at ladies using it; but eventually she took the greatest delight in watching the merry cycling parties of princesses which started daily from Balmoral in the autumn, and she enjoyed many of her hearty laughs at those who were in the learner's stage, and had not mastered the mystery of maintaining the balance.

Another of Her Majesty's characteristics which influenced the national life of her own sex was the Queen's love of fresh air and outdoor exercise. There is a connection between the sovereign taking her breakfast in a tent on the lawn and spending many hours of each day driving, whatever the weather may be, and the fine, healthy, well developed girl of the period swinging her tennis racket, playing hockey, and boating and cycling. When the Queen was young such things were not, and the mammas of that time were probably shocked when they first heard, fifty and more years ago (1840's), of Her Majesty going deer-stalking with her husband for nine hours at a stretch, undertaking perilous mountain expeditions, and walking about in the wilds of Balmoral with a hood drawn over her bonnet to protect her face from the rain. She was fond, too, of taking an early walk before breakfast. She always encouraged her daughters to take plenty of outdoor exercise, and they were expert skaters at a time when the pastime was an uncommon one for ladies.

Princess Alice was a particularly graceful skater, and after her marriage found that she was nearly the only lady in Darmstadt who could skate. [1]

Golf was also enjoyed by ladies on both sides of the pond. It became a popular sport among women in the 1890s. *Godey's Lady's Book* was quite adamant about the proper costume for this sport:

The fancy suits sold in the shops are quite unsuitable for resisting the wear and tear which the inveterate golfer must inevitably encounter. She must not be afraid of a little rain or modicum of mud and should wear thick laced boots either black or tan, with broad low heels, or shoes with leather or cloth legging reaching to her knees. A suit of stout Scotch tweed or English homespun in small checks or mixed color-ings is the best choice: it is made with a rather short and well-fitted skirt, a Norfolk or Eaton jacket, or an open fronted coat: a stiff shirt or a shirt waist is worn beneath, and an alpine or tam of the same material as the gloves, covers the head. A covent coat or a silk lined golf cape is necessary to put on after finishing the game, as one is always heated.

One wonders how they could have played at all once they were suitably dressed.

Two developments of the Victorian era helped to spawn a new game called lawn tennis. One was the lawn mower, which allowed almost everyone to have a cut patch of grass, and the other was the vulcanization of rubber, which made rubber tennis balls possible.

In 1874 Walter Clopton Wingfield invented the new game of lawn tennis. At last young men and ladies had a legitimate reason to cavort around on the lawn together, socializing while they were playing the exciting game. By the 1890s almost everyone was enjoying the new leisure activity.

In April 1898, the U.S. Congress declared war on Spain, which was described by some as "a great little war." Many people began to feel it was the country's Christian duty to be imperialistic. It was also a time of social unrest. Union and management waged bloody battles. Cox's army marched to Washington, and women demonstrated for the right to vote.

A year later, Britain was involved in the Boer War in South Africa. Victoria was reportedly "strongly opposed to making war on the South African Republic and the Orange Free State." [2] She did not want to live the remaining years of her life with a cloud of war hanging over her country. She longed for the rest that peace brings to the soul.

For those in America who wanted to forget about the unpleasant events of war, there was the wildly popular theater. In 1900 there were more than 2,000 theaters in the country. America was entertained by everything from comedy routines to dog acts. There were also top attractions such as Ethel Barrymore, Enrico Caruso, and Harry Houdini. George M. Cohen's talent filled theaters with music and the hearts of people with song.

The most revolutionary form of transportation during this time period was the automobile. It began as a novelty for the rich and succeeded in changing the entire world.

The 1893 Columbian Exposition

Throughout the 19th century, expositions and exhibitions played a unique role in the development of art and industry. In 1893 Chicago was the host city for the World's Columbia Exposition. The event was planned to celebrate the 400th anniversary of the discovery of America. Countries from all over the world were represented.

The real star of the show was the new and exciting entity of nature known as electricity. "A more wonderful, magical sight was never seen than that revealed by the marvelous displays of electrical apparatus, machinery, and devices made in the Electric Building." The *Columbian Exposition Album* included this description:

The interior of the Electricity Building, either by day or night, but especially at the latter time was a place to conjure by. Crackling sparks—lightning in the miniature—flew from buzzing dynamos. Luminous balls of ever changing colors chased one another along cornices, up pillars, and round corners;

mysterious automatic wands traced iridescent words and erased them again with a magic touch; and the voices of far-off singers were heard as if nearby, echoed from the Atlantic Coast along conducting wires. It was a wonderland, the enchanted throne room of Electra.

Although the Centennial Exposition included a Women's Building, the Columbian Exposition had "the first full complete representation ever accorded to women." Everything produced by women from books to needlework was displayed with pride. Many were amazed at the scope of talents displayed by those of the fairer sex.

Visitors to the fair were exposed to brilliant displays of jewelry, and American jewelers were well represented. Tiffany and Gorham even had their own pavilions. There were displays by 29 jewelry manufacturers from New England, which were joined by other companies from all over the world who were showing their finest pieces. Tray after tray of rings, chains, bracelets, earrings, and watches provided a spectacle of delight. The Venetian Glass Works had its own building. Thirty Venetian artists could be seen at work making mosaics, etchings, and blown-glass items. The jewelry was not only an attractive addition to the wardrobe, but it also provided a nice souvenir of the fair.

The Queen's Diamond Jubilee

On Sunday, June 20, 1897, the thanksgiving services held in all parts of the British Empire, as well as in all lands without its borders where Englishmen were gathered together, formed a fitting prelude to the great national celebration of the Diamond Jubilee. A nation felt that Queen Victoria's reign had brought manifold blessings not upon the British Empire only, but upon the whole race of man; that the lofty standard of public duty developed in the United Kingdom during the sixty years, due in no small degree to the personal influence of the venerable Sovereign, had leavened the thought of the whole civilized world. It had sunk deep into the hearts, not of the democracy of England only and of the great kindred democracy across the Atlantic, but of all the rulers and states-men of the Old World.

The quiet ceremony of an unofficial and almost of a family character at which the Queen herself assisted was most interesting.

This quote was written by the Rev. John Rusk, who witnessed the ceremony and the spectacle of the procession that preceded and followed it. The procession was filmed, allowing us to see for the first time a moving picture of the short, overweight queen dressed in black and wearing a white headdress sitting in her Cinderella-like horse-drawn gold carriage, as well as the throngs of people who lined the streets waving scarves and handkerchiefs while they shouted and cheered the good queen.

The Diamond Jubilee was a special occasion for Victorians. As often was the case, souvenirs of the celebration were in order. Merchants met this demand with a multitude of choices, many of them in the jewelry category. Brooches and pins in every price range were made and sold.

This is one of the least expensive pieces worn to commemorate the Diamond Jubilee. Note the pin is attached by a safety pin attachment. Even though the safety pin had been patented a number of years earlier, it didn't become popular as a pin assembly until the 1890s. The safety pin-type head is often found as a catch on an inexpensive brooch of the period.

Victoria's subjects could not have picked a more appropriate choice than jewelry. It was always the gift of choice for the queen. She had been given jewelry on every important occasion of her life and had lavishly given jewelry to her husband, children, and friends.

Another inexpensive pin worn to celebrate the Diamond Jubilee.

Fashions in Clothing and Jewelry

Clothes had begun to slim down in 1887, and the slimming continued into the 1890s. By June 1891 *Peterson's Magazine* was happy to report that "everything has slimmed down even more but the sleeves have ballooned out giving a 'butterfly' silhouette to the feminine frame."

As the clothing slimmed, so did the jewelry. Earrings became small and dainty, set with diamonds, white sapphires, or crystals, many of which were set in buttercup mountings.

Necklace and matching earrings, circa late 1880s-early 1890s. Note the squarish girdle outline of the old mine-cut stones. In 1891 a bruting machine was developed that allowed diamonds to have a round girdle outline. $800

FINE SOLID GOLD EAR DROPS.

Prices per Pair.

No. 4973.....$4 75
Heavy mountings,
white brilliant.

No. 4974.....$3 50
Heavy mountings,
white brilliant.

No. 4975.....$3 00
Blue steel color,
brilliant.

No. 4976.....$2 00
White brilliant.

No. 4977.....$1 88
White brilliant.

No. 4978.....$1 50
Blue steel color,
brilliant.

No. 4980.....$3 50
Heavy mounting,
fine brilliant.

No. 4981.....$2 75
Heavy mounting,
fine brilliant.

No. 4982.....$2 00
1 carat stone,
golconda gem.

No. 4983.....$1 00
White brilliants.

No. 4984.....$3 00
Ruby doublet.
No. 4985.....$3 00
Emerald doublet.
6 brilliants.

No. 4986.....$3 75
Ruby doublet.
No. 4987.....$3 75
Fine emerald
doublet.

No. 4990.....$7 00
Fine opals.

No. 4991.....$5 00
Fine opals.

No. 4992.....$3 25
Fine opals.

No. 4993.....$2 38
Fine opals.

No. 4994.....$1 75
Fine opals.

No. 4995.....$3 25
Fine white roman
pearls.

No. 4997.....$2 00
14k. without backs,
stone settings.

No. 4998.....$1 88
10k. with backs,
stone settings.

No. 4999.....$1 88
10k. with backs,
stone settings.

No. 5000.....$1 75
Real stone center.

No. 5061.....$1 68
Roman flower,
bright cut,
stone center.

No. 5002.....$1 50
Real stone settings.

No. 5004.....$1 17
Garnet settings.

No. 5005.....$1 08
Engraved.

No. 5006.....$1 00
Engraved.

No. 5007.....$1 34
Cube.

No. 5008.....$1 17
Cube.

No. 5009.....$1 75
Facetted ball.

Earrings from a wholesale Otto Young Co. catalog from 1901. These prices are wholesale, per pair.

Lavalieres were ideally suited for soft clothing. These dainty pendants with the popular baroque pearl dangle remained popular through the 1920s.

DIAMOND MOUNTED GOLD LOCKETS.
SOLID 10K GOLD. Prices Each.

Lockets became small and dainty in the 1890s. They were available in gold, gold-filled, gold- plated, silver, gunmetal, and silver-plated. Most of them were engraved with the owner's initials in a fancy script scroll on the reverse. Remember that these are from a wholesale catalog. The ones shown in this illustration are in 10k gold.

DIAMOND MOUNTED GOLD LOCKETS.
SOLID 10K GOLD. Prices Each.

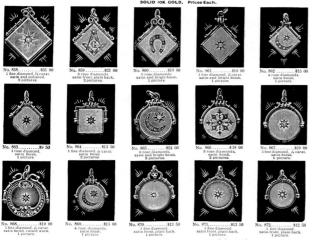

These styles of lockets were often used as fobs on watch chains during this time period.

The increase in women's activities led to changes in wardrobe. Because bicycling was a favorite pastime, clothing materials were chosen with this fact in mind. In 1896 *Godey's* stated, "For Cycling, the stitched alpines (a hat) of English cloth or of felt are greatly used; they stand any amount of wear and tear and are very comfortable. Young girls are wearing cycling costumes of white pique or mohair. The former possesses the advantage of laundering easily, the latter are only suitable for certain occasions, such as a tea, or for wear at fashionable summer resorts."

With the hands busily engaged in keeping the cycle on the road, coin purses were attached to a chain and worn around the neck. Watches and lorgnettes were also worn in this manner. It is interesting to note that chains were rather long, so long that when sitting, the attached articles usually rested in the lap.

Jewelry Box Antiques (D)

Bangles were very popular throughout this time period. They were made in a variety of styles and metals. Many of the bangles that have survived are gold-filled. These gold-filled examples are priced from $200 to $289.

The whistle bracelet was another popular bicycling accessory. It was a "protective ornament" for women who took long rides by themselves. The shrill whistle could be heard for a distance of two miles, used to summon help in case of an emergency. The police also used whistles to alert the public that a crime was in progress so everyone knew to respond to the shrill noise.

Hats were an intricate part of any wardrobe and designed in a variety of styles. Russian turbans and English box turbans "with crowns matching the suits and bordered with fur or feather ruching" were popular. The October 1896 issue of Godey's stated, "Oceans of plumes will be greatly worn. Creme felt hats with trimmings of the same color are stylish for evening wear. Dainty capotes of bright-hued velvet studded with gems or embroidered in gold are the proper thing for the theater."

Royalty still exerted an influence on fashion. As late as 1891, Queen Victoria's approval affected a fashion's acceptance. The Ladies' Home Journal confirmed this in its fashion suggestions for October: "Long sleeves will continue in fashion during the winter, and the women who like delicate lace ruffles falling down over their hands and making them look so small, may indulge in this fancy, and not only have the knowledge that they are in good taste, but also that it is a fashion approved by the Queen of England."

Alexandra, Prince Edwards's wife, also exerted an influence on fashions in clothing and jewelry. Because Alexandra was young and attractive, she influenced fashion even before she became queen. High necklines and collars complemented her long, graceful neck. Realizing this, she wore them frequently. This started a fashion that prompted an 1896 Godey's Lady's Book to note, "High neck dressing is in the rage just now, a neck band of velvet or ribbon about two and a half inches being the regulation depth. In order to increase the height, a pleating of silk or ribbon, growing narrower in front and extremely high and flaring at the back, is sewn on the inside of the band."

For evening, Alexandra favored choker-type necklaces or "dog collars." Soon women all over England, Europe, and America were wearing them. Pearls were another of her favorites. This made them even more desirable to the general public.

Princess Alexandra

Prince Edward also had an influence on fashions in clothing and jewelry. He is said to be responsible for setting the fashion for creased trousers. His love of horse racing helped make good luck symbols and all sorts of horseracing paraphernalia popular as motifs for jewelry and charms.

In 1890 Charles Danna Gibson introduced his illustrations of the Gibson Girl. She became the personification of the ideal and she was definitely what we would call today a woman with attitude. Young ladies of all social levels tried to emulate the style and grace of the Gibson Girl. It's interesting to note that the famous Mr. Gibson was the great-uncle of Charlie Gibson, host of ABC's "Good Morning America."

No. 5326.....$2 17
7 imitation brilliants.
Roman.

No. 5327.....$2 17
9 fine
imitation diamonds.

No. 5328.....$1 63
Polished,
9 pearls.

No. 5329.....$0
Polished.

A few styles of gold scarf pins and stickpins. Prices are wholesale.

This young woman illustrates the attitude and stance made popular by the Gibson Girl. Note where she is wearing her hinged bangle bracelet with the center cameo. She is also wearing a cameo ring.

MADE BY
BATES & BACON,
ATTLEBORO, MASS.

No. 32
PATENTED

Polished, Roman, Old English and Satin.

Made in seven sizes—5, 5¼, 6, 6⅜, 6¾, 7¼, inches in circumference, inside measurement.

YOU WANT the "BATES" BRACELET

SEE OTHER SIDE

The front page of a small catalog shows the Bates and Bacon "Kant Kum Off" styles. They were advertised to be designed "with no visible joint or catch, easy to put on or take off—just a slight pull and a twist, yet it will not unfasten when on the arm." Look carefully at every bangle, so if you encounter one like this you do not damage it by trying to pull it apart the conventional way.

Hearts were a favorite motif during this era. They were found on bracelets, necklaces, rings, and all types of pins and brooches.

Number 882 BRACELET.
This handsome lady's bracelet is made of the best gold plate of extra quality. The top is engraved in a very graceful design and is the grandest value ever offered. It has a catch with which to open it and a safety guard which prevents you from losing it.
Sample, by mail..................$1.75

Number 884 BRACELET.
This elegant misses' bracelet is made of extra quality of the very best gold plate. It opens and closes with a catch. The top is beautifully engraved and you cannot tell it from a solid gold bracelet.
Sample, by mail..................$1.45

Number 885 BRACELET.
This is a very heavy gold filled lady's bracelet, quality guaranteed. The top is beautifully engraved, and it opens and closes with a catch. Each one comes in a silk moreen bag, and is the very best value in the world.
Sample, by mail..................$2.00

Number 889 BRACELET.
This fine lady's bracelet is made of rolled gold plate warranted. It is very heavy with the top beautifully engraved. It opens with a slight twist at the joint and will fit any size arm.
Sample, by mail..................50 cents
One Dozen, by mail..................$4.75
One Dozen, by express..................4.70

Number 890 BRACELET.
This lady's bracelet is electro gold plate of the best quality. The entire bracelet is beautifully engraved and it has a signet top. It opens with a slight twist at the joint, and will fit any size arm.
Sample, by mail..................25 cents
One Dozen, by mail..................$2.75
One Dozen, by express..................2.65

Number 1026 BRACELET.
This handsome bracelet is gold plated and can be adjusted to fit any size arm. It is beautifully engraved and is set at the top with a very fine heart-shaped amethyst.
Sample, by mail..................75 cents
One Dozen, by mail..................$7.00
One Dozen, by express..................6.75

Number 1027 BRACELET
This beautiful lady's bracelet is gold filled; warranted to be of the very best quality. You cannot tell it from solid gold. It is finely engraved, has a signet top and can be adjusted to any size arm.
Sample, by mail..................$1.00
One Dozen by mail..................$10.50 | One Dozen, by express..................10.25

Address J. LYNN & CO., 48 BOND STREET, NEW YORK.

All styles of bracelets were popular. This mail order catalog is one from which the author's grandfather often shopped. Note the top bracelet is gold electroplated but is referred to as gold plate. The fourth one down is rolled gold and much more expensive. The fifth bracelet from the top is a patented "Kant Kum Off" bracelet by Bates and Bacon.

No. 2971. $4.00
Sterling silver, heavy, real stones in hearts.

No. 2972. $2.75
Sterling silver, fancy ornamentation.

No. 2967. $2.50
Rolled plate.
No. 2968. $2.50
Sterling silver, keyless lock.

These bracelets are priced at wholesale for each piece.

No. 2947. $22.50
Plain Bracelet, fancy hearts

No. 2950. $18.00
Plain Bracelet, fancy hearts.

These bracelets are priced per dozen.

Brooches and pins also slimmed down to suit the styles of the day. Small safety-pin-like pins were used for ladies' cuffs and also were scattered on the lace bodices of dresses. Even horizontal pins with endearing terms for babies had become smaller and more delicate looking.

Opals had lost much of their bad luck connotation and were now considered mystical and magical. They were used to embellish all types of jewelry because their play of color was fascinating.

The *Ladies' Home Journal* for October 1891 described the following brooch set with an opal: "An oddity, that cannot fail to inspire comment, is a lace pin representing a vulture about to seize a fluttering bird from its nest. The vulture is of rich gold with an oblong Opal inserted in its back, while its victim is of diamonds and emeralds." This may sound a little gruesome for today's society, but it was a desirable piece in its time.

The assortment shown here is not only a good example of popular ring styles of the day but also illustrates the relative value of the stones. It is interesting to note that a ring of turquoise was a few dollars more than the same ring set with opal, while prices for French turquoise (a fake stone) were only a few dollars less than a fine opal.

Diamonds were very popular. They had not as yet become the epitome for engagement rings because birthstones were still considered the favorite stone choice for that occasion. But the very wealthy favored the diamond as a status symbol, and the new middle class did its best to emulate them as much as possible.

As you can see from the accompanying illustrations, the mountings came in a variety of styles and scales.

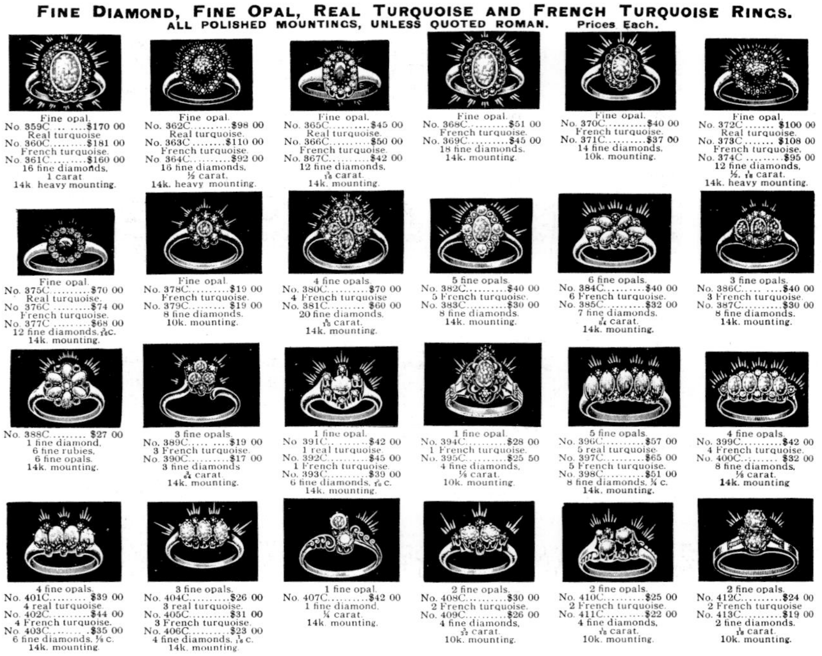
FINE DIAMOND, FINE OPAL, REAL TURQUOISE AND FRENCH TURQUOISE RINGS.
ALL POLISHED MOUNTINGS, UNLESS QUOTED ROMAN. Prices Each.
Fine opal. No. 359C........$170 00 Real turquoise No. 360C.........$181 00 French turquoise. No. 361C.........$160 00 16 fine diamonds, 1 carat 14k. heavy mounting.
Fine opal. No. 362C.........$98 00 Real turquoise. No. 363C........$110 00 French turquoise. No. 364C.........$92 00 16 fine diamonds, ½ carat. 14k. heavy mounting.
Fine opal. No. 365C.........$45 00 Real turquoise. No. 366C.........$50 00 French turquoise. No. 367C.........$42 00 12 fine diamonds, 3/16 carat. 14k. mounting.
Fine opal. No. 368C.........$51 00 French turquoise. No. 369C.........$45 00 18 fine diamonds. 14k. mounting.
Fine opal. No. 370C.........$40 00 French turquoise. No. 371C.........$37 00 14 fine diamonds. 10k. mounting.
Fine opal. No. 372C.......$100 00 Real turquoise. No. 373C.......$108 00 French turquoise. No. 374C.........$95 00 12 fine diamonds, ½, 1/16 carat. 14k. heavy mounting.
Fine opal. No. 375C.........$70 00 Real turquoise. No. 376C.........$74 00 French turquoise. No. 377C.........$68 00 12 fine diamonds, 3/16 c. 14k. mounting.
Fine opal. No. 378C.........$19 00 French turquoise. No. 379C.........$19 00 8 fine diamonds. 10k. mounting.
4 fine opals. No. 380C.........$70 00 4 French turquoise No. 381C.........$60 00 20 fine diamonds. 5/16 carat. 14k. mounting.
5 fine opals. No. 382C.........$40 00 5 French turquoise. No. 383C.........$30 00 8 fine diamonds. 14k. mounting.
6 fine opals. No. 384C.........$40 00 6 French turquoise. No. 385C.........$32 00 7 fine diamonds. 7/64 carat. 14k. mounting.
3 fine opals. No. 386C.........$40 00 3 French turquoise. No. 387C.........$30 00 8 fine diamonds. 14k. mounting.
No. 388C.........$27 00 1 fine diamond, 6 fine rubies, 6 fine opals. 14k. mounting.
3 fine opals. No. 389C.........$19 00 3 French turquoise. No. 390C.........$17 00 3 fine diamonds 3/64 carat. 14k. mounting.
1 fine opal. No. 391C.........$42 00 1 real turquoise. No. 392C.........$45 00 1 French turquoise. No. 393C.........$39 00 6 fine diamonds, 3/16 c. 14k. mounting.
1 fine opal. No. 394C.........$28 00 1 French turquoise. No. 395C.........$25 50 4 fine diamonds, ⅛ carat. 10k. mounting.
5 fine opals. No. 396C.........$57 00 5 real turquoise. No. 397C.........$65 00 5 French turquoise. No. 398C.........$51 00 8 fine diamonds, ¼ c. 14k. mounting.
4 fine opals. No. 399C.........$42 00 4 French turquoise. No. 400C.........$32 00 8 fine diamonds, ⅛ carat. 14k. mounting
4 fine opals. No. 401C.........$39 00 4 real turquoise. No. 402C.........$44 00 4 French turquoise. No. 403C.........$35 00 6 fine diamonds, ⅛ c. 14k. mounting.
3 fine opals. No. 404C.........$26 00 3 real turquoise. No. 405C.........$31 00 3 French turquoise. No. 406C.........$23 00 4 fine diamonds, 1/16 c. 14k. mounting.
1 fine opal. No. 407C.........$42 00 1 fine diamond, ¼ carat. 14k. mounting.
2 fine opals. No. 408C.........$30 00 2 French turquoise. No. 409C.........$26 00 4 fine diamonds, 3/32 carat. 10k. mounting.
2 fine opals. No. 410C.........$25 00 2 French turquoise. No. 411C.........$22 00 4 fine diamonds, 1/16 carat. 10k. mounting.
2 fine opals. No. 412C.........$24 00 2 French turquoise No. 413C.........$19 00 2 fine diamonds. 1/16 carat. 10k. mounting.

Otto Young Wholesale Jewelry Co. catalog, 1901.

It was not long before the automobile began to influence fashion. A dustcoat with a belted or buttoned waist was a necessity. The Marvin Smith Company of Chicago listed several "automobile styles ladies' rain coats" and "ladies and misses automobile Mackintoshes" in their catalog. Scarves that covered the hat and tied under the chin were essential for women, and goggles were a must.

Popular Stones

Alexandrites

New stones were being used in jewelry. "Like canines, every stone has its day," noted the *Ladies' Home Journal* in 1891. "At present, the Alexandrite appears to be in the ascendancy. This jewel comes from Siberia, and is of a beautiful dark green transparent color, which under any artificial light changes to that of pigeon blood ruby. The Alexandrite is cut like a diamond and is being used by the leading jewelers for lace pins, bracelets, and other ornaments."

Remember that a true alexandrite changes from green to red, *not* from blue to purple as does the manmade synthetic alexandrite-like corundum, which is so often mistaken for the real thing.

Moonstones

Moonstone is a type of translucent feldspar. It was so named because of the blue-white sheen that seems to glow from within. Some moonstones are colorless; others have a pearly look. They are even found as moonstone cat's eye.

The moonstone was a popular stone in the 1890-1917 period. It filled the designer's need for a nearly colorless stone, and its moonish glow added a mystical touch to any piece it adorned.

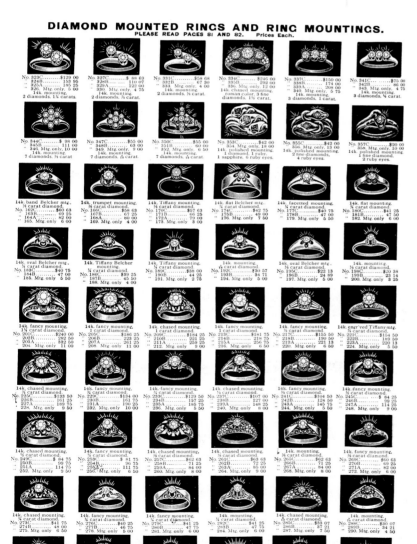

DIAMOND MOUNTED RINGS AND RING MOUNTINGS.
PLEASE READ PAGES 81 AND 82. Prices Each.

Another page from an Otto Young catalog. While they may seem like a bargain to us, keep in mind that these rings were priced wholesale and were still a tremendous amount of money for the average working-class buyer.

The Ladies' Home Journal for October 1891 described two pieces of jewelry set with moonstones:

> A bewitching little moonstone cherub flying with outstretched wings through a garland of gold leaves, intermingled with diamonds and sapphires, forms an exceedingly pretty brooch design that has been imported from Paris.

> A carved moonstone in the midst of diamonds set to simulate stars, for the ornamentation of plain gold concave cuff links, is in Vogue.

Because the stone is a symbol of the moon, it had romantic associations. Like the moon, it symbolized love, romance, and passion. Many felt that it had powers of persuasion in these areas. Some Victorians believed that if you gave someone a piece a jewelry containing a moonstone, you would then have control of the wearer's heart. Others believed that if you put a moonstone under your tongue on the night of a full moon, you would be able to tell the future. Consequently, the moonstone was a favorite stone to give a sweetheart. The moonstone is also one of the birthstones for June.

Moonstone pin-pendant given to the author by her husband, Michael. "It worked! I married him," she said. $1,200.

Moonstone brooch and bracelet, both set in silver.

Peridot

Because of its olive green color, the mineralogical name for peridot is olivine. It is not uncommon to find yellow-green or even brownish peridots.

Peridots have been mined for more than 3,500 years on the small island of St. John in the Red Sea. Other mines are located in Burma, Bohemia, Norway, Australia, Brazil, and South Africa. In the United States, peridots are found in Arizona, New Mexico, and Hawaii.

Peridot is fairly soft and tends to be brittle, but a table- or emerald-cut stone mounted in yellow gold is quite beautiful.

The magical properties ascribed to the peridot include the powers to overcome timidness. King Edward VII considered the peridot his good luck stone. His preference made it popular throughout his reign.

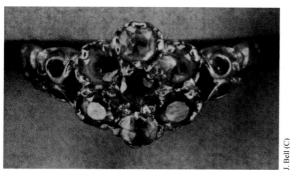

Peridot ring in 15k gold. $550.

A 14k gold lavaliere set with peridot and pearls. This photo also shows another view of the preceding peridot ring. $650.

Demantoid Garnet

A lesser-known variety of the garnet group is the demantoid (deh-MAN-toid). Its rich emerald green color and diamond-like luster make it the most valuable of garnets. The Victorians often miscalled it olivine. Although a deposit of demantoid was found mid-century, it wasn't known as demantoid until the late 1870s. It was most popular in the last quarter of the 19th century and especially in the last decade of that time period. The mine in the Ural Mountains of Russia was exhausted by about 1905, and consequently a demantoid garnet is very expensive. Demantoids can often be identified by their horse-tail-like inclusions.

Bohemian Garnets

The first section of this book focused on gemstones and materials that were destined to be popular throughout the Victorian period. One of these was the garnet. The most popular of the garnet varieties was what was referred to as the Bohemian garnet. This is the color of the garnet group from which the stone gets its name, meaning "glowing coals." Its warm, rich deep color assured its acceptance by all ages in every level of society. Many of the motifs were used over and over again, but the scale of the pieces varied to suit the times and fashions.

Keeping with the scale of the clothing, garnet jewelry also became lighter. The illustration here is from a wholesale jewelry catalog and amply illustrates the popular styles of this time period.

Popular motifs in garnet jewelry from 1890-1910.

Jewelry Box Antiques (D)

Garnet jewelry, $250-$400.

Pearls

Pearls are formed in mollusks. They begin when a tiny irritant enters the oyster, which reacts by secreting a substance called nacre (NAY-kur) to surround the intruder. The gradual buildup of this substance creates the pearl.

Pearls were a favorite of Queen Alexandra, and women throughout the ages have prized the gems. A visit to most any art museum will prove this fact with portrait after portrait of women wearing pearls with pride. They were used for necklaces, bracelets, earrings, and rings, and were sometimes even sewn onto dresses for decoration.

The Oriental pearl is the most desirable. It does not necessarily come from the Orient, but derives its name from the luster associated with pearls from that region. They are always formed by nature in seawater. The ones of highest quality are found in the Persian Gulf.

Freshwater pearls are found in rivers all over the world. Between 1896 and 1899, pearls valued at over a half million dollars were found in the White River in Arkansas. Pearls are also found in edible clams and oysters, but these usually lack the luster of the more valuable ones.

Pearls come in many shapes and sizes. When a pearl becomes attached to the wall of a shell and forms a flat back, it is called a button pearl. Blister pearls are another malformation, and the name provides an apt description. Blister pearls and button pearls are quite lovely when set in earrings, brooches, and rings. Another malformed pearl is known as the baroque pearl. It was perfect for art nouveau jewelry designs and made the ideal appendage for the lavalieres that were so popular

Amber

Amber beads were popular during the 1890-1917 period. Amber is fossilized tree resin. More than 50 million years ago trees taller than the redwoods of today grew along the shores of the Baltic Sea. The movement of the glaciers during the ice age swept the trees into the sea. There they solidified under ice and pressure. Scientists believe that the trees probably had a fungus of some type because the resin was so loose it even surrounded dewdrops. Amber often has insects, petals of flowers, seeds, and bark locked inside. These add to the value of the gem.

One of the oldest gems known to man, amber has been revered through the ages. The Greeks called it "lectron," which is the root word for electricity. Ancient man wore it for protection against disease. As recently as the 1920s, doctors melted amber and mixed it with honey to make a remedy for throat ailments. People even believed that wearing an amber necklace would cure a goiter.

Although light yellow (honey colored) is the color most commonly associated with the name, it can also be brown or red (cherry amber). Color varies according to the depth of water into which the tree fell. Amber can be translucent, opaque, or a mixture of both.

Amber has a very distinct feel. The best way to become acquainted with it is to actually handle a piece. It is so lightweight that long, beautiful strands can be worn with ease.

Amber is not only a lovely accessory, but it can be a good investment. It can be worn with a feeling of safety

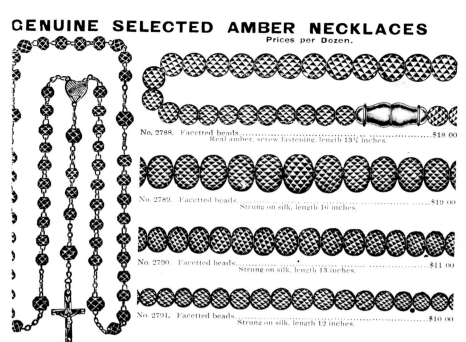

GENUINE SELECTED AMBER NECKLACES
Prices per Dozen.

No. 2788. Facetted beads..$18 00
Real amber, screw fastening, length 13¼ inches.

No. 2789. Facetted beads..$19 00
Strung on silk, length 16 inches.

No. 2790. Facetted beads..$11 00
Strung on silk, length 13 inches.

No. 2791. Facetted beads..$10 00
Strung on silk, length 12 inches.

Rosaries.
2793. Amber beads....$22 50
2794. Garnet " 22 50
r plated wire and ornaments.

The Otto Young wholesale catalog featured amber beads by the dozen.

J. Bell (C)

Sterling silver watch beautifully decorated with gold and niello. $1,100.

no longer associated with diamonds. When buying amber, as with any fine gem, always deal with a reputable source. To ensure its beautiful luster, take care to protect it from hairspray and perfume. A bath in warm water and gentle detergent will keep it sparkling clean.

Enamel

It is not surprising that jewelry designers in this time period made use of ancient enameling techniques. The scope and range of enameling could produce an endless variety of effects. One color of enamel could be applied on top of another to create the varied, flowing colors so indicative of the period. Colors could be opaque or transparent. The possibilities were unlimited, and enamel's durability made it suitable for everyday use.

Plique-a-jour (pleek-ah-ZHOOR) is an enameling method that was used to full advantage by art nouveau designers. It is an especially delicate method in which the enameling has no backing, only sides. To achieve this feat, the enameling mixture is used in a molasses-type form. Sometimes a thin metal or mica backing is used and removed after firing. The designer Cellini used a layer of

clay to back his pieces while firing. Whatever material is used, the results are quite lovely. The enamel has the effect of stained glass or gemstones. These translucent enamels are seen at fullest advantage when held to the light.

Niello (nee-EL-oh) is considered a form of enameling even though it is not a true enamel. A mixture of sulfur, lead, copper, or silver is used instead of the powdered glass enamel. After the design is engraved in the metal, the niello mixture is applied. The piece is fired and then polished to remove the niello from all but the incised portion of the design. Black niello is easy to distinguish from black enameling because it lacks sheen and has a metallic look.

Guilloche

The French word "guilloche" is a term used to describe the beautiful patterns made by a rose-engine-turning lathe and covered with translucent enamel that reveals the pattern underneath. This method was employed extensively by Carl Faberge and other designers of the time period. Guilloche was sometimes embellished with painted enamel designs as seen on the locket here.

Jewelry Box Antiques (D)

Silver locket with guilloche background and painted enamel embellishment. Some damage. $350.

Popular Materials

Celluloid

A marvelous new artificial plastic made from pyroxylin and camphor made it possible for people of modest means to have combs, bracelets, necklaces, and brooches that looked much more expensive than they actually were. Celluloid, the trade name given this material by its inventor, John Wesley Hyatt, in 1869, was widely used in the 1890-1917 period. Combs that looked like tortoise, bracelets and necklaces that could pass for ivory, and pins of every description were made from celluloid. In December 1896, *Godey's Lady's Book* included an article on gifts for Christmas. It recognized the affordability of celluloid items:

> *Much less expensive are the neat celluloid goods, either silver mounted or adorned with a small miniature or cameo head; here again twenty-five cents to a dollar will purchase much that is attractive in the way of trinket sets, little fancy boxes, trays, pocket combs, brushes, and mirrors.*

Because celluloid was highly flammable, its use in jewelry manufacturing was discontinued when safer plastics became available. Since celluloid jewelry was made for a limited time, these pieces will become more collectible and increase in value. At the present time, however, good bargains can still be found.

Paintings on Porcelain

Though not technically a material, painting on porcelain was so popular during this time period that it shouldn't be left out of this section.

Jewelry Box Antiques

Some examples of paintings on porcelain. $65- $125.

Because of new labor saving devices and better working hours and conditions, people had more time to explore leisure activities, and this included hobbies such as painting flowers, portraits, and scenes on porcelain that could be made into brooches and earrings. Limoges plaques in round, oval, square, and rectangular shapes could be purchased along with the hardware that could be glued onto them to transform them into earrings or brooches. This hobby became so popular that the finished pieces became somewhat the fashion. Companies also started producing paintings on porcelain. Many of the examples produced at home or in a factory had a gold band of paint around the outer edge of the plaque.

Some pieces that appear to be paintings on porcelain are really transfers or decals—pictures printed on a clear backing and transferred onto a plaque. These can usually be identified by the tiny dots that are visible under magnification. Some transfers on porcelain were augmented with paint strokes that rise above the surface of the plaque to give the appearance of a painting.

Popular Metals

Platinum

One of the heaviest, most valuable metals known to man, platinum was first discovered in 1557 by Julius Scaligerk, an Italian scientist. In the 1700s Spanish explorers discovered deposits in Peru and called it "plata," their name for silver.

Platinum was the premium metal for jewelry in this time period. It was used very little until the late 1880s. At that time, new developments in jeweler's equipment made it easier to work, and it became popular for mounting diamonds. Platinum's durability made it an excellent choice for the lacy, openworked mountings that were popular about 1900.

The same ore that yields platinum contains five other metals—iridium, palladium, rhodium, ruthenium, and osmiridium. These are known as the platinum group; of these, platinum, palladium, and rhodium are widely used in jewelry.

German Silver, Nickel Silver, Gunmetal

The term "German silver" is a misnomer. German silver is not silver at all, but rather a combination of nickel,

copper, and zinc. A German introduced it to England in the late 1700s. Because its color resembles silver, it made a perfect base for silver-plated items, hence the name German silver. To confuse matters even more, it is also known as gunmetal or nickel silver. When a piece is marked E.P.N.S., it is electroplated nickel silver.

This painting on porcelain in an oxidized or gray metal frame was probably referred to as German silver gunmetal.

Silver Electroplate

In 1840, G.R. Elkington was granted a patent on a process for electroplating silver or gold to a base metal.

This process uses electricity to apply a coating of silver to an article made of base metal. Although this coating

Silver-plated chatelaine.

J. Bell (C)

is usually very thin, pieces more than a hundred years old are sometimes found in amazingly good condition. The most popular base metals were copper and German silver.

The Death of the Queen

As late as December 1896, *Godey's Lady's Book* noted: "Queen Victoria has just had her picture taken; it is that of a hale and hearty old lady in the perennial white cap; in spite of rumors as to her abdication, the Queen holds the reins of estate with a firm grip, and seems in no haste to hand them over to the still jolly and giddy Prince of Wales."

The fateful news that Victoria, R. I., by the grace of God Queen of the United Kingdom of Great Britain and Ireland, defender of the faith, and Empress of India, was no longer of this life was announced to the world on Tuesday, Jan. 22, 1901, in the following simple bulletin: "Her Majesty the Queen breathed her last at 6:30 o'clock, surrounded by her children and grandchildren." [3]

The news of the queen's death left Great Britain stunned. Most people could not remember a time in which she had not been their queen. Even though they had already turned away from Victorian standards, her physical loss was still incomprehensible.

It was when the cold, gray day dawned that the renewed decline of the vital powers warned the watchers that their struggle against nature could not much longer succeed. The Queen was then completely unconscious, and from moment to moment the exhaustion of the small remaining store of vitality became perceptibly greater. Shortly after 9 o'clock the doctors sent summonses to all the members of the family and also to the rector of the royal chapel.

Before they arrived there took place that prudential phenomenon which nature sometimes grants to the dying. The Queen became conscious and free of all suffering. It was under these circumstances of precious memory that the last interviews with her children and grandchildren took place. The world

will never know, and has no right to know what took place. The Queen received them singly, and by two and three within the next four hours. She recognized most of them. Then the curtain of unconsciousness fell for the last time, and the physicians made known that the Queen was dying. All assembled and remained until the very end. It was so quiet and peaceful and gentle that it was difficult to realize that the shadow of death was present.

Nothing more can be said of those last moments. Even the dazzling light which beats upon a throne did not penetrate that chamber, and the tender memories of the last hours belong to those who mourn Victoria, not as a Queen, but in the dearer relationship of family. None of the royal family left the grounds of Osborne House on Friday, and the King had no other occupation than performing reverent offices for the dead. About 10 o'clock in the morning the shell was brought into the bedroom, where were waiting King Edward, Emperor William, the Duke of Connaught, Sir James Reid, and the royal ladies. The latter having retired, Sir James Reid, with reverent hands, assisted by three trusted household servants, and in the presence of the King, the Emperor, and the Duke, removed the body from the bed to the coffin. In death it was lovelier than in the closing days of life. Not a trace of the ravages of disease was visible. [4]

The queen was buried in the Royal Mausoleum located on the grounds of Frogmore house. Before their marriage, Albert had decided to be buried in a Gothic style mausoleum to be built in Coburg. After marrying Victoria, he and the queen decided to erect their own resting place. Shortly after the death of Albert, the queen decided on the site and the interior ornamentation done in the style of Raphael, who was Prince Albert's favorite artist.

Marble effigies of Prince Albert and Queen Victoria were made after Albert's death. At the end of Victoria's long life, no one remembered where her statue had been stored. After some investigation, an old staff member recalled where Victoria's statue had been stored through the years. Victoria's effigy was created at the same time that Albert's had been made. Their marble statues lie together at the tomb, forever frozen in time.

The End of an Era

This photo of the queen was taken in 1897. In it she poses in the same manner as in her last photo, which was taken in 1899. Both photos indicate that she still enjoyed wearing her jewelry. On her right arm she wears a bracelet containing a miniature of her beloved Albert turned so that the entire world could see.

Photo of Queen Victoria taken in 1897, from the book The Beautiful Life and Illustrious Reign of Queen Victoria *by the Rev. John Rusk.*

In both photographs Queen Victoria seems to be in a pensive, contemplative mood, staring out in a side view pose. She looks as if she is contemplating the world and how different it had become in the years since she was a girl of eighteen who had accepted the responsibilities of being queen.

Her world had changed from one composed mostly of farmers to one filled with factories, machines, railroads, and instant communications. In Buckingham Palace she even had a telegraph set up to communicate with India.

Queen Victoria had experienced these new things firsthand and marveled at them. She had ridden one of the first trains; sent one of the first telegraphs; delighted in the machinery at the exhibitions; and even ridden in one of the early steam-driven cars.

The average person could not only have their photograph taken at a relatively inexpensive price, but they could now own a camera. Cameras were the rage since George Eastman had made the box camera available to the general public. The queen was often photographed, and at last her loyal subjects could see what she really looked like at close range.

By 1901 Kodak had some competition as these advertisements from McClure's Magazine *illustrate.*

Music boxes now brought music into the homes.

Advertisement for the Regina music box from McClure's Magazine.

Even the middle class could now enjoy indoor plumbing, although the queen had enjoyed the pleasure for years.

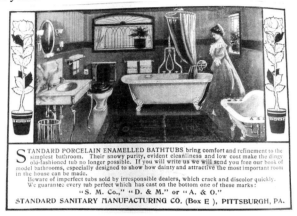

Bath advertisements from the same magazine.

Automobiles operated on batteries, steam, and even gasoline. The Toledo steam carriage advertises that even "a woman can operate it."

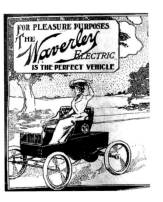

Mail-order catalog companies had sprung up. People could now enjoy shopping from their home. They could purchase anything from a dress to a piano through the mail.

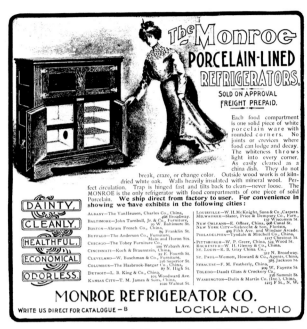

Even a refrigerator could be purchased through the mail, with the seller pre-paying the freight.

A souvenir pin commemorates Victoria's life. This inexpensive pin has her image on the front and the dates of her birth, coronation, marriage, and death on the reverse.

McClure's Magazine from 1901 advertised these automobiles.

A portion of a painting of Victoria presenting a Bible. The painting not only signifies Victoria's earnest concern with spreading religion to all people, but her belief that Prince Albert was always with her even after his death. Although the portrait was created several years after his death, he was painted into the background at the queen's request. Note the bracelets that she is wearing.

a tradition of decorating Christmas trees, which quickly spread to the United States. Her examples set standards and rules of behavior that are still followed by many today.

At Victoria's death, Prince Edward became Edward VII. His coronation was also celebrated with souvenir jewelry.

A souvenir bracelet features a photograph of the late Queen Victoria and a coin commemorating the new king and queen.

Indeed it was a different world!

Queen Victoria's death not only ended her life, but it ended a *way* of life—one that had seen the rise of art and industry in Great Britain and a restored regard for the monarchy.

Victoria had prided herself on bringing religion to the uneducated.

By example, the queen had placed family and home in the forefront of Victorian life. She and Albert started

Edward VII reigned from Victoria's death in 1901 until his death in 1910, thus truly ending the Victorian era.

Both of these advertisements from London stores feature coronation brooches.

Colored fashion plate from August 1902. These young ladies may well represent the last generation with any memories of Victoria as queen of Great Britain.

A bust simply titled "The Queen."

The Fashions

Here are some fashions taken from women's magazines of the era. *Graham's Magazine*, *Peterson's Magazine*, and *Godey's Lady's Book* were popular magazines throughout the 19th century. Then we will visually explore the jewelry that was used to accessorize these fashions.

Peterson's Magazine *fashions from June 1891. There is no sign of the bustle, but look at the mutton sleeves and the drop front waist.*

The Designer, *November 1898. You can tell that these women—even though they're dressed in winter coats—are wearing less clothing than had been worn by women since the beginning of the century.*

Another fashion page from the November 1898 issue of The Designer. *Don't these women look smart?*

Hats for November 1898 look as if they could just fly off the wearer's head. Two hats have wings and two have feathers.

McCall's Magazine, *March 1900, "Ladies' Visiting Costumes."*

McCall's Magazine, *March 1900, "Ladies' Promenade Costume."*

This advertisement for corsets reveals the secret of how women achieved small waistlines.

THE DOWAGER

THE DOWAGER CORSET is *the best corset for stout figures ever manufactured.*
It is worn by thousands of women, and unqualifiedly endorsed by them as

The Most Stylish and Comfortable, Best-Fitting and Durable

Pricing Section
1890s

Bracelets

Jewelry Box Antiques (D)

Two bracelets, circa 1890s, yellow gold-filled, hinged bangle, signet style.
Price: $289 citrine glass, $249 amethyst glass

Photo courtesy Sotheby's of London 12-16-03 (A)

Bracelet, circa 1890s, gold and diamond hinged bangle set with a cushion-shaped diamond weighing 5.58 cts. set between split gold shoulders, approximately 54 mm diameter.
Price: $22,680, £12,600

Photo courtesy Sotheby's of London 12-16-03 (A)

Bracelet, circa 1890s, gold, hinged bangle, decorated at the front with cushion-shaped sapphires and circular-cut diamonds, approximately 55 mm diameter.
Price: $1,512, £840

Photo courtesy Bonhams and Butterfields 6-23-03 (A)

Bracelet, 18k gold, Victorian, hinged bangle top prong-set with old European-cut diamonds; estimated total diamond weight: 4.95 cts., size 7-1/8".
Price: $4,700

Photo courtesy Sotheby's of London 12-16-03 (A)

Bracelet, circa 1890-1900, gold serpent, designed as a series of supple woven gold coils, the eyes set with faceted rubies, French assay marks.
Price: $2,160, £1,200

Bracelet, circa 1890s, gold in quartz.

Sue Brown (D)

Price: $2,700, £1,500

Jewelry Box Antiques (D)

Bracelet, circa 1890s, yellow gold-filled, woven crossover style.

Price: $225

Messada Antiques (D)

Bracelet, circa 1890s, oval bangle, diamond center set with pearls.

Price: $3,537, £1,965

Two bracelets, circa 1890s, yellow gold-filled, hinged bangle, one engraved, one plain.
Price: $295 engraved, $269 plain

Jewelry Box Antiques (D)

Bracelet, circa 1890, moonstone, double heart motif.
Price: $2,520, £1,400

Messada Antiques (D)

Photo courtesy Skinner 9/23/03 (A)

Bracelet, Edwardian, 14k gold mounting set with sapphire and diamonds, hinged bangle bezel-set with three old European-cut diamonds alternating with two circular-cut sapphires, approximate total diamond weight: 1.16 cts.

Price: $3,525

Photo courtesy Skinner 9/23/03 (A)

Bracelet, Edwardian, 14k gold mounting set with opals and diamonds, prong-set with seven graduating opal cabochons interspersed with fourteen old mine-cut diamonds, approximate total weight: 2.10 cts., completed by a bracelet of expandable links (with two additional links).

Price: $2,488

Photo courtesy Skinner 9/23/03 (A)

Jewelry Box Antiques (D)

Bracelet, platinum, 14k gold yellow, gold mesh body, designed as a coiled snake, head set with old European-cut diamond weighing approximately 1.01 cts., rose-cut diamond eyes offset by dark platinum, 1g., 11-1/2", stamped "PD."

Price: $7,050

Bracelet, circa 1890-1910, sterling silver with heart lock clasp and two teeth. (Victorians loved teeth and claws from all types of animals.)

Price: $275

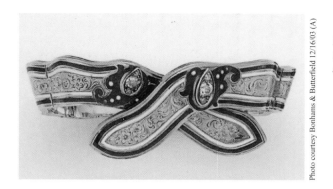

Photo courtesy Bonhams & Butterfield 12/16/03 (A)

Bracelet, 14k gold, flexible, hinged bangle designed as undulating ribbon, overlapping in front, accented by European-cut diamonds, surface decorated with white and rust- colored enamel, size 6 1/2".

Price: $1,200

Bracelet, 14k gold, double-hinged bangle designed as a coiled snake, body in blue basse-taille enamel, seed pearl accents and red stone eyes, 14.0 dwt. (damage to enamel).

Price: $1,410

Photo courtesy Skinner 3-16-04 (A)

Jeanenne Bell (C)

Bracelet, hinged bangle, centered with oval amethyst, embellished with pearls.

Price: $1,800

Jeanenne Bell (C)

Bracelet, circa 1890-1910, sterling silver with coins made throughout reign of Queen Victoria.

Price: $150

Jewelry Box Antiques (D)

Bracelet, circa 1890-1910, sterling silver with heart lock and monogrammed clasp, 7" long.

Price: $350

Brooches

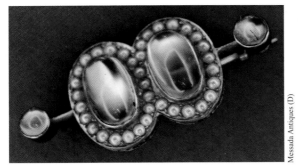

Brooch, circa 1890s, 15k gold, moonstones with pearls.

Price: $1,400, £780

Messada Antiques (D)

Brooch/pendant combination, circa 1890s, peridot and half pearls, 2".

Price: $1,610, £895

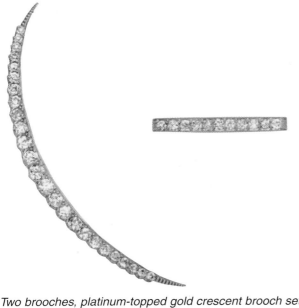

Photo courtesy Bonhams and Butterfields 6-24-03 (A)

Two brooches, platinum-topped gold crescent brooch set throughout with old European-cut diamonds, estimated total diamond weight: 3 cts., together with a platinum bar brooch set with European-cut diamonds, estimated total diamond weight for the lot: 4 cts.

Price: $ 2,644

Photo courtesy Bonhams and Butterfields 6-22-03 (A)

Brooch/pendant, Victorian, platinum-topped 12k gold, star burst design, centering a European-cut diamond weighing approximately 1.45 cts., rays set with old European- and mine-cut diamonds, with removable pin back, estimated total diamond weight: 8.25 cts.

Price: $4,994

John Joseph (D)

Back view of brooch.

Brooch, circa 1890s, wings of love set with diamonds and pearl, love token, 2-1/2" wide.

Price: $4,500, £2,500

Photo courtesy Bonhams and Butterfields 6-22-03 (A)

Brooch, circa 1890, platinum-topped gold, designed as flowers tied with looping ribbons, set throughout with European- and old single-cut diamonds, estimated total diamond weight: 5.4 cts.

Price: $2,644

Messada Antiques (D)

Brooch, 18k gold, granulation work, 1-1/8" diameter.

Price: $1,188, £660

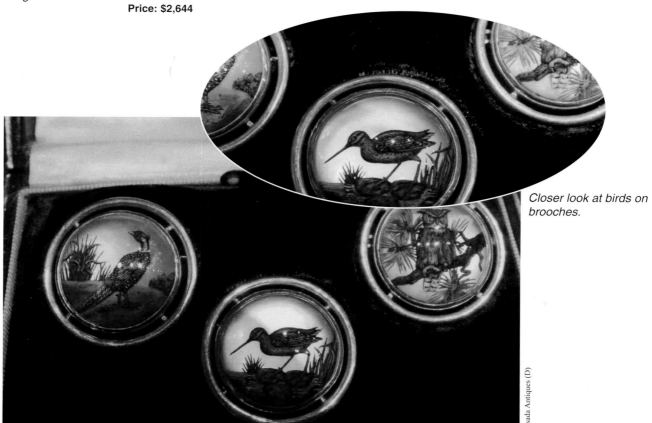

Closer look at birds on brooches.

Messada Antiques (D)

Set of three brooches, Charles Essex, mother of pearl, cutout crystal, reverse painting, remounted in France in 1890s, 1-1/4" diameter.

Price: $13,050, £7,250

Brooch, circa 1890, double hearts surrounded by seed pearls, 2" x 1/2".

Price: $612, £340

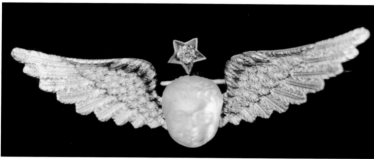

Brooch, circa 1900, diamond and carved moonstone, three-color gold and platinum wings.

Price: $4,549, £2,700

Brooch, circa 1890s, gold Scottish thistle mounting, 1-1/2" x 1".

Price: $765, £425

Brooch, circa 1890s, gilded silver dragonfly, 2-1/4" x 2-1/2".

Price: $1,150

Brooch, circa 1890s, dragonfly motif, plaque a jour with rhinestones, approximately 1-1/2" x 1-1/2".

Price: $950

Old World Jewelry (D)

Brooch/pendant, circa 1890s, silver over gold, 9k gold chain, opal heart motif.

Price: $2,900

Veritas (D)

Closer view of opal.

Back view of opal.

John Joseph (D)

Brooch/pendant, circa 1890s, French Medusa cameo with diamond, 2-1/4" x 1".

Price: $1,620, £900

Sue Brown (D)

Brooch, circa 1890s, square, pietre dure Florentine inlay.
Price: $1,417, £840

Jeanenne Bell (C)

Brooch, 14k gold, set with amethyst and pearls, 3" x 1/4".
Price: $675

Jewelry Box Antiques (D)

Brooch, circa 1890s, yellow gold-filled, enamel.

Price: $325

Side of brooch showing safety pin clasp.

Brooch, circa 1890s, oval butterfly, pietre dure Florentine inlay.

Price: $1,417, £840

Sue Brown (D)

Photo courtesy Bonhams & Butterfield 9/23/03 (A)

Brooch, circa 1900, diamond and platinum-topped gold crown, set throughout with European- and old European-cut diamonds, estimated total diamond weight: 4.30 cts.

Price: $4,700

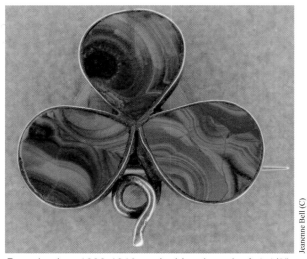

Brooch, circa 1890-1910, malachite clover leaf, 1-1/8" x 1-1/8".

Price: $110

Jeanenne Bell (C)

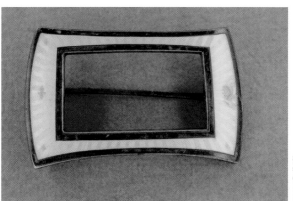

Brooch/sash pin, circa 1890-1910, sterling silver, oval shape, 2-1/8" x 3-1/8".

Price: $300

Jeanenne Bell (C)

Brooch/sash pin, circa 1890-1910, sterling silver top, 2" x 3".

Price: $400

Jeanenne Bell (C)

Brooch, circa 1890-1910, painted enamel on basse taille, 1-1/2" x 1-7/8".

Price: $95

Jeanenne Bell (C)

Brooch, circa 1890-1910, transfer with hand-painted augmentation, 2-7/8" x 1-3/4".

Jeanenne Bell (C)

Price: $175

Brooch, circa 1890-1910, transfer on porcelain embellished with hand-painted gold border, 2" x 1".

Jeanenne Bell (C)

Price: $239

Brooch, circa 1890-1910, enamel on copper, 1-3/8" x 2".

Jeanenne Bell (C)

Price: $195

Brooch, circa 1890-1910, sterling silver horseshoe (GOOD LUCK), 1-1/8" x 1".

Jeanenne Bell (C)

Price: $110

Earrings

Photo courtesy Bonhams and Butterfields 3-24-03 (A)

Earrings, circa 1900, silver-topped 14k gold, Russian, each silver-topped gold earring suspending a round pendant set with mine-cut diamonds, topped by two collet-set diamonds, completed by a euro-lever back; estimated total diamond weight for the pair: 1.30 cts.; hallmarks from Odessa, Russia.

Price: $1,116

Lockets

Inside view of locket.

Jewelry Box Antiques (D)

Locket, circa 1880-'90s, sterling silver, money holder, hand-engraved, 2-1/2" x 3-1/4".

Price: $350

Code by photograph credit line:

(A) Auction House—Auction Price

(C) Collector—Collector Asking Price

(D) Dealer—Dealer Asking Price

Jewelry Box Antiques (D)

Locket, circa 1880-'90s, 14k gold monogram, two compartments for photos, 1-7/8" x 1-3/8".

Price: $495

Jewelry Box Antiques (D)

Locket, circa 1880-'90s, yellow gold-filled set with brilliants, 2-1/2" x 2".

Price: $240

Locket, circa 1880-'90s, yellow gold-filled with monogram "AJA," 1-3/8" x 1".

Price: $95

Locket, circa 1880-'90s, 10k gold monogram "H," 1-3/4" x 1-7/8".

Price: $395

Locket, circa 1880-'90s, yellow gold-filled, 1-1/4" x 1-3/8".

Price: $89

Locket, circa 1880-'90s, yellow gold-filled, engine turned, face with shield, 1-5/8" x 1-1/4".

Price: $110

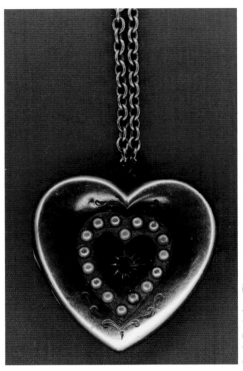

Locket, circa 1880-'90s, heart shape on original chain, approximately 1-7/8" x 1-7/8", chain is approximately 24" long.
Price: $160

Jewelry Box Antiques (D)

Two lockets, circa 1890s; 9k gold with diamond, 1"; 10k yellow gold, monogram, 1-1/4".
Price: $325 (9k), $375 (10k)

Jewelry Box Antiques (D)

Necklaces

Closer view of necklace.

Necklace, circa 1890, rare neck chain by Master Jeweler Guiliano, England's most famous jeweler, moonstones with enamel backings in between.
Price: $14,760

Sue Brown (D)

Compartment in back for hair.

Necklace, circa 1880-'90s, heart pavé set with pearls, bottom drop detachable.

Price: $5,310

Necklace, circa 1890s, demantoid garnets and opals.

Price: $1,975

Necklace, circa 1880-'90s, seed pearls with diamond in the middle.

Price: $6,210, £3,450

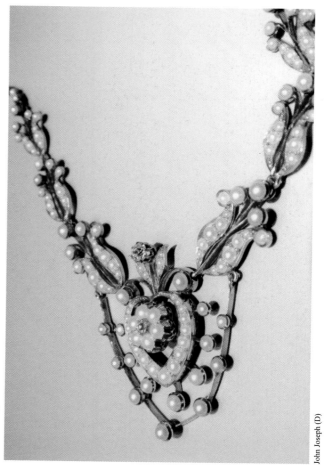

John Joseph (D)

Messada Antiques (D)

John Joseph (D)

Necklace, circa 1880-'90s, gold over brass, 164 rose-cut garnets, 1.72 mm x 4.1 mm.

Price: $1,195

Jewelry Box Antiques (D)

Necklace/coin holder, circa 1890s, gunmetal.

Price: $300

Michael Sher (D)

Necklace, circa 1890s, demantoid garnets and pearls.
Price: $4,500, £2,500

John Joseph (D)

Necklace with tiara attachment, circa 1900, platinum-topped gold necklace of knife-edge design with graduated, fringe-style drops set with European- and mine-cut diamonds, completed by detachable knife-edge chains set with collet-set diamonds; accompanied by a silver and gold tiara attachment of later date; estimated total diamond weight: 5 cts.; necklace 14-1/2" long.

Price: $8,813

Photo courtesy Bonhams & Butterfields 9/23/03 (A)

Pendants

John Joseph (D)

Pendant/drop, circa 1890s, amethyst and seed pearls, 2" x 1".

Price: $1,250, £695

John Joseph (D)

Pendant/necklace, circa 1890s, amethyst and seed pearls, 3" x 1-1/4".

Price: $2,520, £1,400

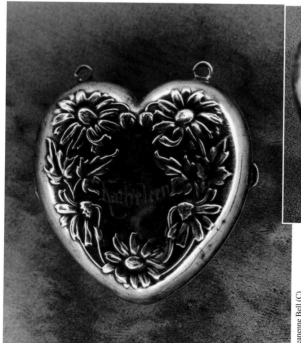

Jeanenne Bell (C)

Pendant/locket, circa 1890s, sterling silver, heart motif, opens to reveal slots for coins.

Price: $400

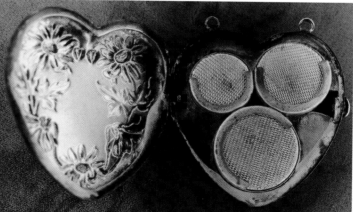

Open view of locket.

Pendant coin holder, circa 1890, silver-plated, round.

Price: $125

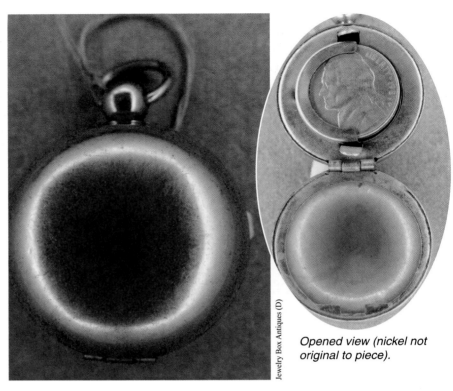

Jewelry Box Antiques (D)

Opened view (nickel not original to piece).

Jeanenne Bell (C)

Back view of pendant brooch showing where pin stem is attached.

Pendant brooch, 18k gold, centered with amethyst and embellished with half pearls, approximately 2" x 1-1/2".

Price: $900

John Joseph (D)

Pendant/necklace, circa 1890s, peridot and half pearls, 1-3/4" x 2".

Price: $5,130, £2,850

Open view of pendant coin holder.

Jewelry Box Antiques (D)

Pendant coin holder, circa 1890, gunmetal, rectangular with turquoise embellishment, 2-7/8" x 1".

Price: $165

Code by photograph credit line:

(A) Auction House—Auction Price

(C) Collector—Collector Asking Price

(D) Dealer—Dealer Asking Price

Pins

Wimpler Antiques (D)

Pin, circa 1890s, 15k pale greenish gold, clover motif, 1-1/4" diameter.

Price: $1,773, £985

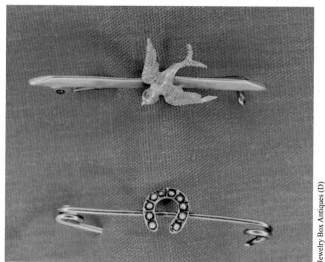

Jewelry Box Antiques (D)

Two pins, circa 1890-1900, 9k yellow gold, horseshoe and bird.

Price: $95 each

John Joseph (D)

Pin, circa 1880-'90s, archery motif, arrows and target, 2" x 5/8".

Price: $890, £495

Photo courtesy Skinner 3-16-04 (A)

Pin, circa 1890s, 14k gold mount, prong-set turquoise cabochon surrounded by old European-cut diamonds, approximate total weight: 1.65 cts.

Price: $1,175

Photo courtesy Skinner 6/17/03 (A)

Pin, silver-topped 18k gold mount, designed as a diamond baton tied with a ribbon, bead-set with fifty-nine old mine-cut diamonds, seed pearl, and millegrain accents.

Price: $646

Renata Ramsburg (D)

Three pins, circa 1890s, (1) lavender enamel, yellow in center with diamond, 1-1/2" x 1-1/2"; (2) violet flower with pearls around it, 1-1/4"; (3) leaf 14k gold, yellow and green, 7/8" x 1".

Price: (1) $2,250, (2) $1,800, (3) $295

Rings

Side view showing one of the hands.

Ring, hallmark 1893, two hands holding two hearts.
Price: $720, £400

Ring, circa 1900, natural cat's-eye alexandrite, diamond and platinum centering an oval cat's-eye alexandrite cabochon weighing 6.98 cts., framed by old European-cut diamonds, estimated total diamond weight: 0.85 cts., accompanied by G.I.A. Gem Trade Laboratory report #10842256, dated Sept. 3, 1999, stating: Natural! Cat's Eye Alexandrite.
Price: $7,050

Ring, circa 1895, 18k gold, centered prong-set pear-shaped opal measuring approximately 14.35 mm x 11.00 mm x 6.10 mm, encircled by European-cut diamonds, the sides and scrolled band embellished by enamel, estimated total diamond weight: 0.85 cts., signed Marcus & Co.
Price: $11,750

Ring, late 19th century, set with circular-cut diamonds in a mount of scrolling decoration, size P-1/2.
Price: $1,836, £1,020

Ring, early 20th century, designed as a floral cluster of cushion-shaped diamonds, size P.
Price: $907, £504

Ring, set with a circular-cut diamond, the center stone weighing 1.77 cts., size L-1/2.
Price: $15,120, £8,400

Ring, 14k gold, centered an old European-cut diamond weighing approximately 1.50 cts., set between two lion heads and paws, size: 9-1/2.

Price: $3,525

Ring, circa 1895, platinum-topped gold set with old European- and old single-cut diamonds, estimated total diamond weight: 1.65 cts.

Price: $4,000

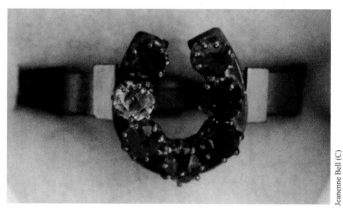

Ring, circa 1890-1910, 10k gold set with black and gray layered agate, small size for child or pinkie finger.

Price: $350

Ring, circa 1890-1910, 15k gold set with green glass and garnet doublets.

Price: $425

Ring, circa 1890-1910, rolled gold horseshoe motif, "REGARDS."

Price: $195

Ring, circa 1890-1910, 18ct gold, English set with peridot, which was Edward, the Prince of Wales' favorite stone.

Price: $650

Watches

Jeanenne Bell (C)

Watch chain, circa 1880-'90s, one row of table-worked hair in two weaves with gold-filled findings and heart-shaped fob, approximately 1/4" x 13-1/2" long.

Price: $165

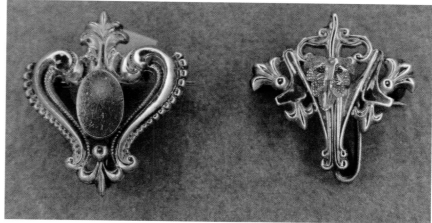

Two watch pins, circa 1890, yellow gold-filled.

Price: $95 (right), $89 (left)

Photo courtesy Bonhams & Butterfield 12/16/03 (A)

Pocket watch, circa 1890; case: 18k yellow gold, circular, open face, hinged, four-bodied, high relief floral motif on back of case, Swiss; dial: white enamel, red Arabic numerals, yellow "Louis XVI" hands; movement: jeweled, lever escapement, cut bi-metallic, screwed balance wheel, adjusted, Breguet balance spring; diameter: 34 mm.

Price: $900

Photo courtesy Bonhams & Butterfield 9/23/03 (A)

Pocket watch, circa 1890, Swiss, retailed in Poland; case: 14k yellow gold, circular, open face, hinged, four-bodied, back of case with applied gold double eagle crest with blue enamel; dial: white enamel, black Roman numerals, sunk auxiliary seconds dial, yellow "spade" hands; movement: gilt, jeweled, lever escapement, cut bi-metallic screwed balance wheel, flat balance spring.

Price: $2,444

Photo courtesy Skinner 6/17/03 (A)

Watch, circa 1895, 18k gold, pair case, Patek Philippe et Cie, white enamel dial with blue Arabic numeral indicators and Louis XV hands, display back enclosing signed movement no. 107961, within blue guilloché enamel case no. 223710 with scene of pink and yellow roses framed by rose-cut diamonds and scrolling vines, outer case with repoussé scene of Hercules, Hebe, and Cupid, dial and movement signed, size 0, together with art nouveau lapel pin bezel-set with a circular-cut sapphire, pearl accent (dial with hairlines).

Price: $9,400

Photo courtesy Skinner 3-16-04 (A)

Pendant watch, 18k gold, guilloche enamel sun burst dial with Arabic numeral indicators, reverse depicting cherub, scrolling rose-cut diamond accents, continental assay mark.
Price: $2,115

Watch, circa 1890-1910, gunmetal with matching watch pin, Swiss with decorated dial.
Price: $700

Jewelry Box Antiques (D)

Jewelry Box Antiques (D)

Watch pin, circa 1890, yellow gold-filled, 1-1/8" x 3/4".
Price: $95

Watch, circa 1880s, 14k, cherub enamel watch, "Remontoir Atroljoie," pin set and stem wind, Swiss lever escapement, hallmarked.
Price: $1,175

Joan Stern (D)

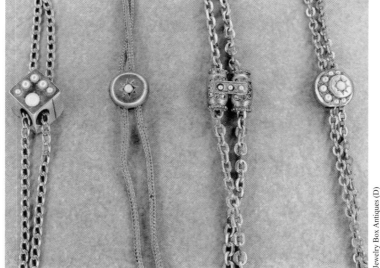

Watch chains, karat gold and gold-filled, slide chains.
Price: $200-$270 gold-filled, $600-$800 karat gold

Jewelry Box Antiques (D)

Miscellaneous and Sets

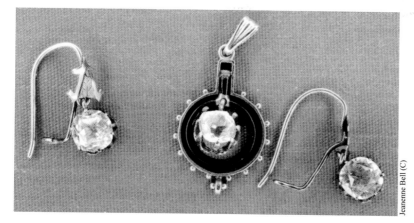

Necklace and earrings, circa 1890s, 14k gold with mine-cut brilliant, pendant 5/8" x 1-1/4", earrings 3/4" long.

Price: $800

Jeanenne Bell (C)

Chatelaine, circa 1890s, 18k gold, each piece French hallmarked, art nouveau motif, purse, mirror, perfume, and knife.

Price: $6,000

Michael Sher (D)

Photo courtesy Skinner 3-16-04 (A)

Code by photograph credit line:

(A) Auction House—Auction Price

(C) Collector—Collector Asking Price

(D) Dealer—Dealer Asking Price

Cuff links, 18k gold, Wise, set with silver denarius depicting a helmeted Roma, signed, partially obliterated French guarantee stamps.

Price: $1,998

Bibliography

Armstrong, Mary. *Victorian Jewelry*, New York: Macmillan Publishing Co., 1976.

Bart, Sir Herbert Maywell. *Sixty Years A Queen*, London: Harmsworth Brothers Publishers Limited.

Becker, Vivienne. *Antique and Twentieth Century Jewellery*, Second Edition, N.A.G. Press Ltd., 1922.

Bell, C. Jeanenne. *Answers to Questions About Old Jewelry*, 6th Edition, Iola, Wis.: Krause Publications, 2003.

Bell, C. Jeanenne. *Collector's Encyclopedia of Hairwork Jewelry*, Paducah, Ky.: Collector Books, 1998.

Bell, C. Jeanenne. *Collector's Encyclopedia of Pendant and Pocket Watches 1500-1950,* Paducah, Ky.: Collector Books, 2004.

Bell, C. Jeanenne. *How to Be a Jewelry Detective*, Shawnee, Kan.: A.D. Publishing, 2000.

Bradford, Ernle. *English Victorian Jewelry*, New York: Robert M. McBride & Co. Inc., 1957.

Bradford, Ernle. *Four Centuries of European Jewelry*, Great Britain: Spring Books, 1967.

Burgess, Frederick W. *Antique Jewelry and Trinkets*, New York: Tudor Publishing Co., 1919.

Bury, Shirley. *Jewellery 1789-1910 The International Era, Volume I, 1789-1861,* Suffolk, U.K.: Antique Collectors' Club Ltd. Publishers.

Bury, Shirley. *Jewellery 1789-1910,* Vol. I & Vol. II, 1991.

Bury, Shirley. *Jewellery Gallery Summary Catalog*, London: Victoria and Albert Museum, 1982.

Clifford, Anne. *Cut-Steel & Berlin Iron Jewelry*, Bath, Great Britain: Adams & Dart Publishers, 1971.

Dietz, Ulysses, Grant; Jselit, Jenna Weissman; Smead, Kevin J.; Zapata, Janet. *The Glitter and the Gold*, Newark, N.J.: The Newark Museum, 1997.

Evans, Joan. *A History of Jewelry 1100-1870*, Boston: Boston Book & Art Publications, 1970.

Flower, Margaret. *Victorian Jewelry*, New York: Duell, Sloan & Pierce Publishers, 1951.

Gene, Charlotte. *Victorian Jewelry Design*, Chicago: Henery Regnery Co., 1973.

Grey, Lieutenant-General C. Compiled under the direction of Her Majesty, Queen Victoria, *The Early Years of His Royal Highness, The Prince Consort*, New York: Harper & Brothers Publishers, 1867.

Hart-Davis, Adam. *What the Victorians Did for Us*, London: Headline Book Publishing Ltd., 2001.

Hibbert, Christopher. *Queen Victoria*, New York: Basic Books, 2000.

Maciver, Percival. *Chats on Old Jewelry and Trinkets*, New York: Frederick A. Stokes Co., 1902.

Rusk, Rev. John. *The Beautiful Life and Illustrious Reign of Queen Victoria*, Boston: James H. Earle Publishers, 1901.

Wilson, Robert. *The Life and Times of Queen Victoria, Volume I,* London: Cassell & Company Publishers, 1887.

Woodham-Smith, Cecil. *Queen Victoria*, New York: Alfred A. Knopf, 1972.

Notes

Section I, 1806-1839

1. *Antiquarium Catalogue*, p.36
2. Clifford, Anne, *Cut-Steel & Berlin Iron Jewelry*, p. 26
3. Bury, Shirley, *Jewellery Gallery Summary Catalog,* Victoria and Albert Museum
4. Bury, Shirley, *Jewellery 1789 -1910*, p. 246

Section II, 1840-1850s

1. Rusk, Rev. John, *The Beautiful Life and Illustrious Reign of Queen Victoria*, p. 148
2. Vox, *The Antiquarium Magazine-2003*, p. 99
3. Bell, C. Jeanenne, *Answers to Questions About Old Jewelry*, 6th ed., p. 10
4. Bury, Shirley, *Jewellery 1789-1910*, p. 21
5. Ibid., No. 4, p. 533
6. Ibid., No. 4, p. 381
7. Ibid., No. 4, p. 380
8. Ibid., No. 4, p. 38

Section III, 1860-1880s

1. Killarney National Park, *The Muckross House*, p. 44
2. Rusk, Rev. John, *The Beautiful Life and Illustrious Reign of Queen Victoria*, p. 229
3. Bell, C. Jeanenne, *Answers to Questions About Old Jewelry*, 6th ed., p. 55

Section IV, 1890-1901

1. Rusk, Reverend John, *The Beautiful Life and Illustrious Reign of Queen Victoria*, p. 453
2. Ibid., p. 370
3. Ibid., p. 377
4. Ibid., p. 377

Index